"The Lies We Live By:

Misinformation, Extremism, and the Threat to Democracy"

This is a work of non-fiction. The events, people, and places depicted in this book are real. Any references to organizations, individuals, or situations are factual, used in context to provide insight into the themes discussed.

First Edition: Sept, 2024

Table of Content:

Preface

In the modern era, democracy faces one of its greatest threats: the proliferation of lies. We live in a time where misinformation spreads faster than truth, where political leaders manipulate reality to serve their own ends, and where extremism is fueled by conspiracy theories that infect public discourse. The lines between fact and fiction have become increasingly blurred, and the consequences of this distortion are profound.

This book, **The Lies We Live By: Misinformation, Extremism, and the Threat to Democracy**, was born out of a growing concern for the future of our democratic institutions. The more I witnessed the rise of political lies, the spread of extremist ideologies, and the manipulation of social media, the more I realized that this is not merely a crisis of information—it is a crisis of trust, of values, and of identity. Democracy, at its core, depends on the ability of citizens to engage in rational, informed debate. But what happens when the very foundation of that debate—truth itself—comes under attack?

Throughout history, societies have wrestled with the challenge of deceit in politics. From the propaganda machines of authoritarian regimes to the manipulative rhetoric of populist leaders, lies have always played a role in shaping political realities. But in today's world, the scale and speed of disinformation have reached unprecedented levels. The digital age, with its promise of connectivity and access to information, has also become a double-edged sword. It has empowered individuals and movements to share ideas but has also provided fertile ground for the rapid spread of falsehoods and dangerous ideologies.

As I began researching this book, I spoke to journalists, historians, political theorists, and activists who are working on the front lines of the battle for truth. Their stories, their insights, and their experiences shaped this narrative. I examined the ways in which political lies have been weaponized—from the manipulation of elections and the undermining of public health efforts to the radicalization of individuals who stormed the U.S. Capitol on January 6, 2021. I looked at how authoritarian regimes have used disinformation to justify human rights abuses, how conspiracy theories have infiltrated mainstream politics, and how the global rise of nationalism has been fueled by falsehoods about immigration, climate change, and more.

This book is not just about diagnosing the problem; it is about exploring solutions. **The Lies We Live By** delves into the efforts of fact-checkers, educators, and ordinary citizens who are fighting back against the tide of disinformation. It looks at how media literacy can be a tool to empower individuals to critically evaluate the information they consume and how technology platforms can be held accountable for the role they play in spreading falsehoods. Most importantly, it is about the need for collective action to reclaim the truth and restore trust in democratic institutions.

This book does not pretend that the path forward will be easy. The challenges posed by misinformation, extremism, and political manipulation are formidable, and the forces that seek to exploit these divisions are powerful. But history has shown that democracies can be resilient if citizens are willing to stand up for their values, hold their leaders accountable, and demand transparency and truth in governance.

I invite you, the reader, to engage with these ideas not just as a passive observer but as an active participant in this crucial battle for the future of democracy. The choices we make today—how we consume information, how we respond to political lies, and how we defend democratic norms—will shape the world that future generations inherit. It is my hope that **The Lies We Live By** serves as both a wake-up call and a guide for navigating the complexities of misinformation in the 21st century.

The truth matters. And it is worth fighting for.

Mark A Conde
Aug, 2024.

Introduction:

The Age of Lies

We live in an era where truth, once considered the foundation of democratic society, has become increasingly malleable. The rise of misinformation has dramatically reshaped the political landscape, undermining trust in institutions, spreading falsehoods, and empowering extremist ideologies. In this age of lies, deliberate disinformation campaigns are not only a tool of manipulation but a powerful weapon wielded to divide, conquer, and control.

In recent years, we've witnessed how falsehoods, amplified through the digital sphere, have influenced elections, fueled xenophobia, and emboldened dangerous ideologies like Neo-Nazism and white supremacy. From the U.S. Capitol insurrection on January 6, 2021, to the rise of nationalist movements across Europe and South America, the consequences of political deceit are all too clear.

Misinformation and the Modern Political Landscape

Misinformation is not new to politics; it has long been used by leaders seeking to consolidate power and shape public perception. However, the scale at which misinformation spreads today, particularly through social media, has turned a once-controlled trickle of lies into an overwhelming flood.

Platforms like Facebook, Twitter, and YouTube serve as the primary vehicles for these false narratives, driven by algorithms that prioritize engagement over truth.

A striking example of this is the 2016 U.S. Presidential Election, where misinformation campaigns—both foreign and domestic—targeted millions of voters. A study by the Oxford Internet Institute revealed how social media played a pivotal role in spreading disinformation, with false stories often outperforming factual ones. Similarly, in the Brexit referendum, misinformation about the economic and political consequences of leaving the European Union was central to the Leave campaign's success.

This weaponization of misinformation has undermined democratic processes, leaving citizens confused, divided, and, in many cases, radicalized. As we will explore throughout this book, the effects of misinformation ripple far beyond the voting booth—they threaten the very fabric of society.

Themes: Political Deceit, Digital Falsehoods, and Extremist Ideologies

This book is structured around three major themes, each connected by the common thread of misinformation:

1. **Political Deceit**: Politicians have always lied, but in today's climate, political deceit has reached unprecedented levels. Leaders not only manipulate

information but also outright deny observable facts, sowing distrust in science, journalism, and democracy itself. In this book, we will analyze how political lies, from Watergate to election fraud claims, have evolved and become central to governance in the digital age.

2. **The Digital Spread of Falsehoods**: The internet was once hailed as the great equalizer, providing access to information for all. However, it has also become a breeding ground for falsehoods. Platforms built to connect people now divide them, as algorithms prioritize sensationalism and misinformation. With insights from experts like Tristan Harris, we will delve into how social media algorithms amplify these dangerous narratives.

3. **The Rise of Extremist Ideologies**: Perhaps the most alarming consequence of misinformation is its ability to fuel extremist ideologies. From Neo-Nazi movements to white Christian nationalism, these groups thrive on disinformation, using it to recruit, radicalize, and spread their hateful messages. We will explore how conspiracy theories like QAnon gain political traction, and how misinformation about immigration and race has emboldened extremist groups around the world.

A Preview of Key Figures, Interviews, and Case Studies

In the pages that follow, we will examine the intersection of misinformation, politics, and extremism through a series of case studies, expert interviews, and real-world examples. Historian Timothy Snyder, in his book *On Tyranny*, reminds us that "post-truth is pre-fascism," a warning that echoes throughout this work. We will hear from journalists like Maria Ressa, who risked their lives to expose the deadly consequences of fake news, and from scholars like Kathleen Belew, who have documented the rise of the modern white power movement.

We will also dive deep into the historical context of political lies, comparing past regimes like Nazi Germany and the Soviet Union to modern political movements. Interviews with former insiders—such as Miles Taylor, author of *A Warning*, and whistleblowers from both corporate and government spheres—will shed light on the mechanics of deceit and disinformation.

Case studies will explore pivotal moments in recent history, from the Brexit referendum to Russian interference in the 2016 U.S. election, as well as the global response to misinformation during the COVID-19 pandemic. These real-world examples illustrate how lies, when unchecked, can fracture societies, fuel extremism, and dismantle democratic norms.

Conclusion

The Age of Lies is not merely a political problem; it is a societal crisis. In this book, we will chart a course through the complex web of deceit, revealing how political lies, digital platforms, and extremist ideologies intersect to threaten the core principles of democracy. This is not just a story of the past but a warning for the future: in the absence of truth, democracy itself cannot survive.

Chapter 1:

The History of Political Deception

P olitical deception is as old as politics itself. From ancient empires to modern democracies, rulers have long recognized the power of controlling information and shaping narratives. Propaganda, lies, and manipulation have been used as tools not just for winning wars, but for maintaining power, controlling populations, and advancing political agendas. In this chapter, we will explore the historical use of political deceit, tracing its roots from the early empires to some of the most infamous regimes of the 20th century. We will also delve into modern-day examples of political deception, revealing how these tactics persist in today's digital age.

The Use of Propaganda and Political Lies Throughout History

Propaganda, the deliberate dissemination of information—often biased or misleading—has been a constant presence in political life. In ancient Rome, emperors like Augustus used monuments, literature, and coinage to promote their divine authority and moral superiority. Similarly, in medieval Europe, monarchs controlled religious narratives to legitimize their rule, framing opposition as heresy or treason.

However, the most notorious and systematic use of propaganda emerged in the 20th century, with the rise of totalitarian regimes. Nazi Germany, under Adolf Hitler, and the Soviet Union, under Joseph Stalin, used propaganda to manipulate the truth, spread disinformation, and consolidate their power. These regimes demonstrated how effectively lies, repeated and reinforced by the state, could shape public perception and justify heinous policies.

Case Study: Nazi Germany and the Power of Propaganda

One of the most infamous examples of political deception is the propaganda machine of Nazi Germany. Joseph Goebbels, Hitler's Minister of Propaganda, orchestrated a campaign that permeated every aspect of German life, from education to the arts, spreading messages of Aryan supremacy and demonizing Jews, communists, and other "undesirable" groups. Goebbels' strategy was simple: repeat a lie often enough, and it becomes the truth.

Nazi propaganda was meticulously crafted to exploit existing societal fears and prejudices. Films like *Triumph of the Will* glorified Hitler and the Nazi Party, while children's books like *The Poisonous Mushroom* spread virulent antisemitism. The regime also controlled the press, suppressing dissent and presenting only the Nazi-approved version of events. The myth of the "stab in the back," which claimed that Germany had been betrayed from within during World War I, was propagated to justify the Nazis' rise to power and subsequent persecution of Jewish people.

The lessons of Nazi propaganda are chillingly clear: when lies are state-sanctioned and unchecked, they can lead to catastrophic consequences. The Holocaust, fueled by racial myths and deception, is a stark reminder of the deadly potential of political lies.

Case Study: The Soviet Union and the Control of Information

In the Soviet Union, deception and control of information were equally integral to the regime's survival. Joseph Stalin's government perfected the art of rewriting history and manipulating facts. Through state-controlled media, Stalin created a cult of personality, portraying himself as the infallible leader of the Communist revolution.

One of the most notorious examples of Soviet deception was the use of doctored photographs. Political opponents of Stalin were systematically erased from historical records, their images literally removed from photographs and their names stricken from official documents. This erasure of history was a form of deception that went beyond simple propaganda—it was an attempt to control reality itself.

The Soviet Union also deployed propaganda to justify its brutal policies, such as the forced collectivization of agriculture, which led to the Holodomor, a man-made famine that killed millions in Ukraine. The Soviet government denied the famine's existence, despite widespread suffering, and used propaganda to blame the victims themselves for their supposed disloyalty to the state.

Case Study: Political Deception in U.S. History

While Nazi Germany and the Soviet Union offer extreme examples of political deception, the United States is not immune to the use of lies and manipulation in its political history. One of the most notable examples is the Watergate scandal, which exposed President Richard Nixon's attempts to deceive the American public and cover up illegal activities.

Nixon's administration engaged in a series of political espionage activities, including the break-in at the Democratic National Committee headquarters. When the scandal broke, Nixon and his aides attempted to deceive the public, discrediting the investigation and denying any wrongdoing. The infamous phrase "I am not a crook" became a symbol of political deceit in the U.S. context.

Another example of deception in U.S. history is the misinformation campaign surrounding the Vietnam War. The U.S. government, under multiple administrations, downplayed the war's escalation and misrepresented the likelihood of success. The release of the Pentagon Papers in 1971 revealed that the U.S. government had systematically lied to the public and Congress about the war's progress and prospects, further eroding trust in political institutions.

Interview with Historian Timothy Snyder: The Link Between Deception and Tyranny

To gain deeper insight into the historical roots of political deception and its implications for modern democracy, we turn to historian Timothy Snyder, author of *On Tyranny*. Snyder's work focuses on the ways in which authoritarian regimes have used misinformation to manipulate the public and erode democratic institutions.

In an interview, Snyder emphasizes the importance of recognizing how post-truth politics can pave the way for tyranny. "Once leaders begin to lie openly, without consequence, they create a reality in which truth is no longer fixed," Snyder explains. "This is the first step toward authoritarianism. If there is no truth, there is no accountability, and power can become absolute."

Snyder draws parallels between the propaganda tactics of Nazi Germany and those used by modern-day autocrats, warning that we are witnessing a resurgence of political deceit on a global scale. "The mechanisms may have evolved—digital platforms, fake news—but the intent is the same: to confuse, to divide, and ultimately to control," Snyder argues.

Conclusion

Political deception is not a relic of the past. From ancient rulers to modern autocrats, the manipulation of truth has been a constant feature of political life. The case studies of Nazi Germany, the Soviet Union, and U.S. political history demonstrate the devastating consequences of unchecked lies and propaganda. As we move forward in this book, we will examine how these historical lessons apply to today's political climate and explore how misinformation continues to undermine truth, trust, and democracy.

Chapter 2:

Misinformation in the Digital Age

T he advent of the internet and the rise of social media have fundamentally transformed how information is disseminated and consumed. While these platforms were initially celebrated for democratizing information and providing a voice to the voiceless, they have also given rise to a new, more insidious form of political manipulation. Social media has become a fertile ground for the spread of misinformation, often amplifying falsehoods far beyond the reach of traditional media outlets. In this chapter, we will explore how digital platforms like Facebook, Twitter, and YouTube contribute to the spread of political misinformation and the consequences this has for society.

The Role of Social Media in Amplifying Political Misinformation

Social media platforms are designed to maximize user engagement, often through algorithms that prioritize content likely to evoke strong emotional responses. While this approach increases user activity and boosts advertising revenue, it also makes platforms vulnerable to the rapid spread of misinformation. Political falsehoods, conspiracy theories, and emotionally charged content are more likely to be shared, commented on, and liked, which results in their further amplification.

Studies have shown that false information spreads faster than the truth on social media. A 2018 study from MIT, published in *Science*, found that false news stories were 70% more likely to be retweeted than truthful ones. This phenomenon is exacerbated by the fact that misinformation often caters to people's biases, fears, or desires, making it more appealing and shareable.

Social media platforms also play a key role in creating "echo chambers," where users are exposed primarily to content that aligns with their preexisting beliefs. These echo chambers intensify polarization, as individuals are less likely to encounter opposing viewpoints and more likely to be exposed to misinformation that reinforces their ideological leanings.

Case Study: Facebook's Role in the Misinformation Ecosystem

Facebook, the largest social media platform in the world, has been at the center of numerous controversies regarding its role in spreading misinformation. During the 2016 U.S. Presidential Election, it was revealed that Russian operatives used Facebook to target American voters with fake news and divisive political ads. According to a report by the U.S. Senate Intelligence Committee, the Internet Research Agency (IRA), a Kremlin-linked group, created thousands of fake Facebook accounts and spread misinformation to sow discord among the American electorate.

Facebook's algorithm, which prioritizes content that generates engagement, played a key role in amplifying this misinformation. The platform's "Groups" feature, in particular, became a breeding ground for conspiracy theories and political falsehoods, as users congregated in echo chambers that reinforced their beliefs. False information about the 2016 election results, immigration, and race relations circulated widely in these groups, reaching millions of users.

In response to growing criticism, Facebook has taken steps to curb misinformation, such as partnering with fact-checking organizations and flagging false content. However, critics argue that these measures are insufficient and that the platform's core business model—driven by engagement—continues to incentivize the spread of misinformation.

Case Study: Twitter and the Viral Spread of Falsehoods

Twitter, while smaller in user base compared to Facebook, has a disproportionate influence on political discourse. It is the platform of choice for many political leaders, journalists, and activists, and its fast-paced, real-time nature makes it a powerful tool for spreading both information and misinformation.

During the COVID-19 pandemic, Twitter became a major platform for the dissemination of false information about the virus, vaccines, and public health measures. Despite efforts by the platform to remove harmful content and flag misleading tweets, misinformation about COVID-19 spread rapidly. A study by the Center for Countering Digital Hate found that just 12 individuals, dubbed the "Disinformation Dozen," were responsible for 65% of anti-vaccine content on social media platforms, including Twitter.

Twitter's retweet and trending features often exacerbate the spread of false information. When users share content, especially tweets that align with their political or ideological views, the platform's algorithm prioritizes this content, making it more visible to others. In politically charged environments, such as during elections or crises, this can lead to the viral spread of misinformation.

Case Study: YouTube and the Rabbit Hole of Misinformation

YouTube, the world's largest video-sharing platform, has also played a significant role in amplifying misinformation. With over two billion users and a recommendation algorithm that suggests content based on user preferences, YouTube can easily lead viewers down a "rabbit hole" of misinformation. A report by the Pew Research Center found that 70% of users watch videos recommended by YouTube's algorithm, often without actively searching for them.

This has proven especially dangerous when it comes to political misinformation and conspiracy theories. A study by Data & Society found that YouTube's algorithm frequently recommended extremist content, leading viewers from relatively innocuous videos to those espousing conspiracy theories, white supremacy, and other forms of misinformation. For instance, users watching videos on conservative politics were often recommended videos from far-right creators promoting falsehoods about immigration, race, and elections.

YouTube has made efforts to combat misinformation by adjusting its algorithm to limit the visibility of content deemed harmful or misleading. However, the platform's recommendation system still prioritizes content that generates high levels of engagement, which can include sensationalist or conspiratorial videos.

Insights from Tristan Harris: The Manipulation of Information Through Social Algorithms

To understand the mechanics behind how digital platforms manipulate information, we turn to Tristan Harris, a former design ethicist at Google and the subject of the documentary *The Social Dilemma*. Harris has become a prominent critic of how tech companies design their platforms to exploit human psychology, keeping users engaged by feeding them emotionally charged content, including misinformation.

In an interview, Harris explains that social media platforms are designed to maximize attention, which in turn maximizes profit. "The longer you spend on these platforms, the more money they make from advertising. And what keeps you engaged? Content that triggers a reaction—whether it's anger, fear, or joy," Harris says. "Unfortunately, misinformation often generates these reactions more effectively than the truth."

Harris argues that social media companies have created a "disinformation economy," where the truth is often a casualty of the drive for profit. "The algorithms don't care about what's true or false. They care about what will keep you scrolling, clicking, and sharing," Harris adds.

Harris also discusses the role of social algorithms in creating filter bubbles, where users are only exposed to information that aligns with their beliefs. This, he warns, leads to greater polarization and makes it harder for individuals to discern truth from falsehood. "When you're only seeing content that confirms your worldview, it becomes much easier to believe in conspiracy theories or false narratives," Harris explains.

Conclusion

In the digital age, misinformation spreads with unprecedented speed and reach, facilitated by the algorithms of platforms like Facebook, Twitter, and YouTube. These platforms, designed to maximize engagement, have become conduits for political falsehoods and conspiracy theories, often with devastating consequences for democratic discourse. The insights of experts like Tristan Harris underscore the need for a fundamental rethinking of how digital platforms operate in the information ecosystem. As we will explore in the chapters ahead, the consequences of unchecked misinformation threaten not only individual understanding but the very foundations of democracy itself.

Chapter 3:

Fake News, Real Consequences

The term "fake news" has become a pervasive part of political discourse, weaponized by leaders and public figures to discredit the media and manipulate public perception. What began as a label for fabricated stories designed to mislead has evolved into a powerful political tool used to undermine trust in legitimate journalism. In this chapter, we will explore the rise of fake news as a political weapon, drawing on interviews with journalists like Maria Ressa, who have been on the frontlines of the battle against misinformation in authoritarian regimes. We will also examine how fake news has influenced elections and global politics, leading to real-world consequences that threaten the integrity of democratic processes.

The Rise of "Fake News" as a Political Weapon

The phrase "fake news" gained widespread attention during the 2016 U.S. Presidential Election, but its roots stretch back much further. Historically, false or misleading information has been used by political actors to gain advantage, smear opponents, and control public opinion. However, the scale and speed at which fake news spreads today, largely due to social media and the internet, have transformed it into a formidable weapon.

One of the most notable examples of fake news influencing political discourse is its use by authoritarian leaders to delegitimize the media. Leaders like Donald Trump in the United States, Rodrigo Duterte in the Philippines, and Jair Bolsonaro in Brazil have weaponized the term to dismiss critical reporting as biased or false, creating an environment where the public becomes increasingly skeptical of the press. In this way, "fake news" is not just a term used to describe fabricated stories but a rhetorical device employed to erode trust in journalism as an institution.

In a study by the Reuters Institute for the Study of Journalism, researchers found that political leaders have been particularly adept at using the fake news label to rally their supporters, painting the media as part of an elite establishment working against the interests of the people. This populist framing of the media as the "enemy of the people" has dangerous implications for the free press, as it encourages hostility toward journalists and diminishes the role of factual reporting in democratic societies.

Interview with Maria Ressa: Battling Misinformation in Authoritarian Regimes

To understand the real-world consequences of fake news, we turn to Maria Ressa, a Filipino-American journalist and founder of *Rappler*, an online news site that has been a critical voice against the authoritarian regime of President Rodrigo Duterte. Ressa's work has made her a target of state-sponsored disinformation campaigns and legal harassment, yet she continues to speak out against the dangers of fake news and the ways in which it is used to stifle dissent and control public narratives.

In an interview, Ressa explains how Duterte's government has used social media to spread disinformation and silence critical voices. "In the Philippines, fake news isn't just a nuisance—it's a weapon of control," Ressa says. "Troll farms, state-sponsored disinformation campaigns, and false narratives are deployed to attack journalists, discredit the opposition, and create an alternate reality where the truth becomes whatever the government says it is."

Ressa, who was awarded the Nobel Peace Prize for her fight against disinformation, stresses the importance of holding social media companies accountable for their role in amplifying fake news. "Platforms like Facebook have become the new gatekeepers of information, but they've abdicated responsibility for the content that spreads on their networks. Without regulation, these platforms are enabling the rise of authoritarianism by allowing fake news to flourish," she argues.

Ressa's experiences highlight the personal dangers that journalists face in environments where fake news is used as a tool of repression. She has been arrested multiple times on trumped-up charges, and *Rappler* has faced significant legal challenges. Yet, she remains committed to exposing the truth, warning that the spread of fake news is not just a threat to journalism but to democracy itself.

Fake News and Elections: A Global Threat

The impact of fake news on elections has been well-documented, with numerous studies showing how misinformation can sway public opinion and influence the outcome of democratic processes. One of the most notorious examples of this is the 2016 U.S. Presidential Election, where Russian operatives spread fake news stories designed to exacerbate political divisions and undermine confidence in the electoral system.

A report by the U.S. Senate Intelligence Committee found that the Russian Internet Research Agency (IRA) created thousands of fake accounts on Facebook and Twitter, disseminating false stories about candidates, voter fraud, and social issues. These fake news stories were often designed to inflame tensions on polarizing topics like race, immigration, and law enforcement. The goal was not necessarily to support one candidate over the other, but to sow discord and weaken the fabric of American democracy.

The consequences of fake news in the 2016 election were profound. A study by the Oxford Internet Institute found that fake news stories were shared more frequently than legitimate news on social media, particularly among groups of highly partisan users. This overwhelming spread of misinformation contributed to a climate of distrust, with many voters believing in false narratives about both candidates.

Fake news has also played a critical role in elections outside the United States. In the 2018 Brazilian election, for example, fake news stories circulated widely on WhatsApp, a messaging platform that is heavily used in Brazil. These stories, which falsely claimed that voting machines were rigged and that left-wing candidates supported criminal gangs, were instrumental in shaping public opinion and ultimately contributed to the victory of right-wing candidate Jair Bolsonaro.

Similarly, during the Brexit referendum in the United Kingdom, fake news about immigration and the European Union spread rapidly on social media, shaping the views of many voters. False claims, such as the widely debunked statement that the U.K. sent £350 million per week to the EU, were central to the Leave campaign's messaging. Despite being proven false, these claims resonated with voters and were repeatedly amplified by fake news outlets and social media campaigns.

Real Consequences: The Erosion of Trust and the Rise of Extremism

The consequences of fake news extend far beyond individual elections. Over time, the constant exposure to false information erodes public trust in institutions, including the media, government, and the electoral system. When people can no longer distinguish between what is true and what is false, it becomes easier for authoritarian leaders to manipulate the public and consolidate power.

This erosion of trust also creates fertile ground for the rise of extremism. In environments where fake news thrives, conspiracy theories and fringe movements can quickly gain traction. For example, the QAnon conspiracy theory, which falsely claims that a secret cabal of elites is involved in child trafficking and satanic rituals, spread rapidly through social media, gaining a significant following in the United States and abroad. QAnon adherents played a prominent role in the January 6, 2021, attack on the U.S. Capitol, a stark example of how fake news and conspiracy theories can lead to real-world violence.

Conclusion

Fake news is not just a nuisance—it is a political weapon that has been used to discredit the media, manipulate elections, and undermine democracy. The experiences of journalists like Maria Ressa, who have fought against disinformation in authoritarian regimes, reveal the personal risks faced by those who challenge fake news. Meanwhile, the widespread influence of fake news on elections around the world demonstrates the far-reaching consequences of this phenomenon. As we will explore in the coming chapters, the battle against fake news is a critical front in the fight to protect democratic institutions and the truth itself.

Chapter 4:

Misinformation and Democracy

Democracy is built on trust: trust in institutions, trust in the electoral process, and trust in the free flow of truthful information. However, in the age of widespread misinformation, this trust is being systematically eroded. The flood of false information—spread through social media, news outlets, and political leaders themselves—undermines democratic institutions and weakens the public's faith in their ability to function. In this chapter, we will explore how misinformation chips away at the very foundations of democracy, drawing on studies from organizations like the Pew Research Center and insights from Steven Levitsky, co-author of *How Democracies Die*.

How Misinformation Undermines Democratic Institutions

The essence of a functioning democracy lies in the ability of its citizens to make informed decisions. When the information that reaches the public is corrupted by falsehoods, however, the integrity of the decision-making process is compromised. Misinformation distorts public perception of key issues, alters voter behavior, and creates confusion around policies, candidates, and elections. This is particularly dangerous in societies where free and fair elections are central to the democratic process, as false narratives can sway election outcomes and disrupt the peaceful transfer of power.

Moreover, misinformation sows distrust in the core institutions of democracy—government, the judiciary, the press, and even the electoral system itself. False claims of widespread voter fraud, for instance, can lead to a loss of confidence in election results, as was evident in the aftermath of the 2020 U.S. Presidential Election. Despite the lack of credible evidence to support claims of widespread fraud, millions of Americans came to believe that the election was "stolen," largely due to the amplification of misinformation through media outlets and social networks.

This erosion of trust in elections is not unique to the United States. Across the globe, misinformation has cast doubt on electoral integrity, from Brazil to Hungary to India. When citizens believe that their vote no longer counts, the very legitimacy of democracy is questioned, and the door is opened for authoritarian leaders to capitalize on public disillusionment.

Studies on Declining Trust in Government

The relationship between misinformation and declining trust in government is well-documented. The Pew Research Center, a leading think tank on public opinion and social trends, has conducted numerous studies highlighting how public trust in government has steadily declined over the past several decades, particularly in the United States.

According to a 2020 Pew Research study, only 20% of Americans said they trusted the federal government to do the right thing "just about always" or "most of the time," down from a high of 77% in 1964. This decline in trust has been exacerbated by the rise of misinformation, which has made it harder for citizens to discern fact from fiction. The same Pew study found that a majority of Americans believe that political leaders, social media companies, and the news media are responsible for spreading misinformation, further eroding trust in these institutions.

One key finding from Pew is that people exposed to misinformation are more likely to view the government as corrupt or incompetent, even in cases where there is little to no evidence supporting such views. This perception of government as inherently untrustworthy leads to disengagement from the political process, as citizens become cynical about the possibility of meaningful change.

The Impact on Democracy: Insights from Steven Levitsky

To gain deeper insights into how misinformation affects democracy, we turn to political scientist Steven Levitsky, co-author of *How Democracies Die*. Levitsky has studied democratic backsliding across the globe and argues that the spread of misinformation plays a critical role in this process. In an interview, Levitsky explains how misinformation weakens the norms and institutions that uphold democratic governance.

"Misinformation is one of the most powerful tools used by authoritarian-leaning leaders to dismantle democracy from within," Levitsky says. "By flooding the public sphere with lies, half-truths, and conspiracy theories, these leaders create confusion and division. This weakens the ability of citizens to hold their leaders accountable, because the truth becomes so obscured that it's hard to know what to believe."

Levitsky points to historical examples of how misinformation has been used to justify undemocratic actions. In Venezuela, for instance, Hugo Chávez's government spread misinformation about opposition leaders, accusing them of plotting coups and destabilizing the country. This narrative allowed Chávez to consolidate power and erode democratic checks and balances under the guise of protecting national security.

In the United States, Levitsky warns that misinformation surrounding election fraud has laid the groundwork for undermining democratic norms. "The 2020 election fraud claims were not just about discrediting an election result; they were about undermining the entire electoral process. When millions of people believe that the system is rigged, it becomes easier for leaders to justify undemocratic measures like voter suppression or even refusing to accept electoral outcomes in the future."

Levitsky's research highlights a disturbing trend: once misinformation takes root in a political system, it becomes increasingly difficult to reverse. Democratic norms—such as the peaceful transfer of power, respect for the rule of law, and the legitimacy of opposition parties—become fragile in the face of relentless disinformation. Leaders who rely on misinformation often portray themselves as protectors of the people, using lies to justify the erosion of democratic principles.

Real-World Consequences: A Fractured Public and Polarized Politics

One of the most significant consequences of misinformation in democracy is the polarization of the electorate. As misinformation spreads, political divisions deepen, making compromise and collaboration between opposing factions increasingly difficult. This polarization is particularly evident in countries like the United States, where partisan media outlets and social media algorithms create echo chambers that reinforce preexisting beliefs and fuel distrust of the "other side."

In a 2021 Pew Research study on political polarization, researchers found that misinformation contributes to the growing ideological divide between Democrats and Republicans. Nearly 80% of Americans said they disagreed with the opposing party not only on policies but on basic facts about the country. This lack of a shared reality makes it nearly impossible to engage in constructive political dialogue or reach consensus on pressing national issues.

Beyond the political sphere, misinformation also affects social cohesion. When people are divided along lines of fact and fiction, trust within communities erodes, and societal bonds weaken. In democracies, where citizens must work together to make collective decisions, this breakdown of trust poses a serious threat to the functioning of democratic governance.

Conclusion

Misinformation is a corrosive force in democracy, undermining public trust in institutions, distorting the electoral process, and contributing to political polarization. Studies from organizations like the Pew Research Center show a clear link between the spread of false information and declining trust in government, while the insights of scholars like Steven Levitsky reveal how misinformation can lead to the erosion of democratic norms. As we will explore in the following chapters, the fight against misinformation is not just a battle for truth but a battle to preserve the very foundations of democracy.

Chapter 5:

Lies in the Oval Office

The Oval Office is the symbolic center of power in the United States, and its occupant wields immense influence over public opinion, policy, and the nation's moral compass. However, the history of U.S. presidential leadership is also marked by moments of deception—when political leaders, for reasons of self-interest or perceived necessity, have misled the public. Misinformation from the highest office can have far-reaching consequences, shaping national discourse, policy decisions, and even the course of history. In this chapter, we will examine how misinformation has been used by U.S. presidents to manipulate public opinion, focusing on key case studies from Richard Nixon's Watergate scandal to Donald Trump's election fraud claims. We will also hear insights from former political insiders like Miles Taylor, author of *A Warning*, who witnessed firsthand how deception operates in the highest levels of government.

The Power of the Oval Office in Shaping Public Opinion

The U.S. president holds a unique position as both the chief executive and the symbolic leader of the nation. When a president speaks, their words carry significant weight, often shaping public opinion and influencing the media's framing of issues. This power, however, can also be used to spread misinformation. A president's ability to control the narrative gives them an unparalleled platform to mislead the public, and when they choose to do so, the effects can be profound.

Historically, U.S. presidents have justified misinformation by framing it as necessary for national security, political survival, or the protection of the public. While some acts of deception may be seen as pragmatic in the moment, the long-term consequences can erode public trust in both the presidency and democratic institutions. Once misinformation is deployed from the highest office, it often cascades through the political system, influencing policy, shaping media coverage, and altering the course of political history.

Case Study: Nixon's Watergate Scandal and the Erosion of Trust

One of the most infamous examples of presidential deception is the Watergate scandal, which led to the resignation of President Richard Nixon in 1974. Watergate began as a political espionage operation—members of Nixon's re-election campaign were caught breaking into the Democratic National Committee headquarters. However, it was the cover-up orchestrated by Nixon and his aides that escalated the scandal into a full-blown constitutional crisis.

Nixon's attempts to deceive the public included the destruction of evidence, the manipulation of federal agencies to obstruct the investigation, and public denials of any wrongdoing. The president's famous statement, "I am not a crook," became a symbol of his administration's attempts to mislead the American people.

The Watergate scandal had far-reaching consequences for public trust in government. It was not just Nixon's deception that was damaging, but the exposure of a broader culture of corruption within the administration. In the years following Nixon's resignation, public trust in the presidency and other institutions plummeted. A 1974 Gallup poll found that only 36% of Americans had confidence in the government, down from 77% in 1964, a sharp decline that was directly linked to the Watergate scandal.

Watergate set a precedent for the media's role in holding political leaders accountable, but it also established a troubling norm: presidents could lie to protect their political interests, even if those lies undermined public trust in the office of the presidency itself.

Case Study: The Iraq War and the Manipulation of Intelligence

Another significant case of presidential misinformation occurred in the lead-up to the 2003 invasion of Iraq. President George W. Bush and his administration justified the war by claiming that Iraq possessed weapons of mass destruction (WMDs) and that Saddam Hussein's regime had links to terrorist organizations like al-Qaeda. These assertions were later proven to be false, but at the time, they were used to rally public and congressional support for the invasion.

The Bush administration's use of misleading intelligence to build a case for war has been heavily criticized. The administration presented selective intelligence reports, downplayed evidence that contradicted their narrative, and exaggerated the threat posed by Iraq. The infamous "16 words" in Bush's 2003 State of the Union address—claiming that Iraq had sought uranium from Africa—became a symbol of the administration's misleading claims.

The consequences of this misinformation were profound. The Iraq War resulted in the deaths of hundreds of thousands of Iraqis and thousands of U.S. service members, destabilized the Middle East, and contributed to the rise of extremist groups like ISIS. It also led to a significant decline in global trust in U.S. leadership and damaged the credibility of American intelligence agencies.

The Iraq War serves as a reminder that presidential misinformation is not just a matter of political maneuvering—it can lead to catastrophic outcomes on a global scale.

Case Study: Trump's Election Fraud Claims and the Attack on Democracy

Perhaps the most recent and significant example of presidential misinformation is Donald Trump's repeated claims of widespread voter fraud during the 2020 U.S. Presidential Election. Despite a lack of evidence, Trump and his allies propagated the narrative that the election had been "stolen" from him, with fraudulent votes cast in key swing states. These claims were rejected by courts, election officials, and independent observers, yet they persisted in the media and among Trump's supporters.

Trump's misinformation campaign culminated in the January 6, 2021, attack on the U.S. Capitol, when a mob of his supporters, incited by his false claims, attempted to overturn the election results by force. This unprecedented attack on the democratic process was a direct result of the spread of misinformation from the Oval Office.

The consequences of Trump's election fraud claims have been long-lasting. According to a 2021 Pew Research Center study, nearly two-thirds of Republicans continue to believe that the 2020 election was fraudulent. This widespread belief in a false narrative has deepened political polarization and undermined faith in the electoral system. The aftermath of Trump's misinformation campaign has raised serious concerns about the future of American democracy, as the peaceful transfer of power—a cornerstone of democratic governance—was called into question.

Interview with Miles Taylor: Inside the Trump Administration

To gain a deeper understanding of how misinformation was used during the Trump administration, we turn to Miles Taylor, a former Department of Homeland Security (DHS) official and author of *A Warning*, who revealed the chaotic and deceptive inner workings of the Trump White House. In an interview, Taylor describes how misinformation was often used as a deliberate strategy to control public perception and deflect criticism.

"There was a constant effort to distort the truth," Taylor recalls. "Whether it was downplaying the threat of COVID-19, exaggerating economic achievements, or pushing baseless election fraud claims, misinformation was a core part of how the administration operated. It wasn't about governing in the traditional sense—it was about maintaining power through whatever means necessary, including lies."

Taylor's experience sheds light on how misinformation became institutionalized within the Trump administration. "What was particularly concerning was how misinformation was normalized," he explains. "People within the administration knew the truth, but there was enormous pressure to go along with the false narratives being pushed from the top. Those who didn't comply were sidelined or forced out."

Taylor's insights reveal the dangers of a presidency that prioritizes misinformation over truth, as well as the long-term damage such practices can inflict on democratic institutions.

Conclusion

From Nixon's Watergate scandal to Trump's election fraud claims, the use of misinformation by U.S. presidents has had serious consequences for public trust, governance, and democracy itself. These case studies illustrate how lies from the Oval Office can shape public opinion, influence policy decisions, and undermine the very institutions designed to uphold democratic governance. As we continue to explore the political landscape of lies, it is essential to recognize the role that misinformation plays in eroding the foundations of democracy and weakening the integrity of the presidency.

Chapter 6:

Brexit and the Lies of Nationalism

T he United Kingdom's 2016 referendum on whether to remain in or leave the European Union, commonly known as Brexit, marked one of the most significant political shifts in recent British history. It was also a key moment in the rise of nationalist rhetoric across Europe, fueled by misinformation and strategic manipulation. The Leave campaign, which successfully advocated for the UK's withdrawal from the EU, was characterized by exaggerated claims, misleading statistics, and emotionally charged appeals to nationalism and sovereignty. In this chapter, we will explore how misinformation shaped the Brexit referendum, focusing on the tactics used by key figures like Dominic Cummings and the broader implications for the UK's economic and social landscape.

The Role of Misinformation in the Brexit Referendum

Misinformation played a central role in the Brexit referendum, particularly in the messaging of the Leave campaign. One of the most infamous examples was the claim that the UK sent £350 million per week to the European Union—a figure that was prominently displayed on the side of a bus and became a key talking point for Leave campaigners. This figure was widely debunked, as it failed to account for the UK's rebate and the funding the country received from the EU in return. Despite being factually incorrect, the £350 million claim resonated with voters who were frustrated with what they perceived as excessive contributions to the EU.

Another significant aspect of the Leave campaign's misinformation strategy was its focus on immigration. The campaign framed the referendum as a way to "take back control" of the UK's borders, capitalizing on concerns about the perceived influx of immigrants, particularly from EU member states. The Leave campaign's messaging often blurred the lines between legal EU migration and broader anxieties about refugees and asylum seekers, creating a narrative that immigration was out of control and that leaving the EU was the only way to address this issue.

The use of misinformation in the Brexit referendum was not limited to financial figures and immigration statistics. The Leave campaign also stoked fears about the future of the UK if it remained in the EU, suggesting that the country's sovereignty was at risk and that EU regulations were eroding British identity. These messages were designed to tap into nationalist sentiments, appealing to voters' sense of patriotism and a desire to reclaim control over national decision-making.

Interview with Dominic Cummings: The Manipulation of Information

Dominic Cummings, the campaign director of Vote Leave, played a pivotal role in shaping the misinformation strategy that defined the Brexit referendum. In an interview reflecting on the campaign, Cummings acknowledged the deliberate use of emotionally charged messaging and exaggerated claims to sway voters. "We knew that facts and statistics alone wouldn't win this referendum," Cummings explained. "What mattered was appealing to people's emotions—especially their fears and frustrations."

Cummings highlighted the importance of digital platforms like Facebook in disseminating the Leave campaign's messages. "Social media allowed us to target specific groups of voters with tailored messages," he said. "We could focus on the issues that mattered most to them, whether it was immigration, sovereignty, or the economy. It was about creating a narrative that resonated emotionally, even if that meant simplifying or exaggerating certain points."

Cummings also discussed the challenges faced by the Remain campaign, which struggled to counter the Leave campaign's emotionally driven messaging. "The Remain campaign focused too much on facts and technical details," he argued. "They failed to connect with voters on an emotional level. Meanwhile, we were telling a simple, compelling story: 'Take back control.'

That message was powerful, even if it wasn't always backed by the most accurate information."

The Economic and Social Impact of Brexit: A Reality Check

While the Leave campaign's use of misinformation helped secure a victory in the referendum, the long-term economic and social consequences of Brexit have been far more complex and damaging than the campaign's rosy projections suggested. Numerous studies have shown that Brexit has had significant negative effects on the UK's economy, trade relationships, and social cohesion.

One of the most immediate impacts of Brexit was the sharp decline in the value of the British pound following the referendum result, which led to increased inflation and higher prices for goods and services. A 2019 study by the London School of Economics (LSE) found that Brexit had already cost the UK economy around £130 billion in lost output, with long-term projections suggesting that the UK could be as much as 6.4% poorer in the years following Brexit compared to a scenario in which the country remained in the EU.

Trade has also been significantly affected by Brexit. The UK's decision to leave the EU's single market and customs union created new barriers to trade with Europe, the country's largest trading partner. According to a 2021 report by the UK Office for Budget Responsibility (OBR), Brexit is expected to reduce the

UK's total trade by about 15% in the long run. British businesses, particularly in the manufacturing and agricultural sectors, have struggled to adapt to new customs procedures, supply chain disruptions, and increased costs.

Socially, Brexit has exacerbated divisions within the UK. The referendum result revealed deep rifts between different regions, age groups, and socioeconomic classes. A 2017 report by the National Centre for Social Research found that Brexit had significantly polarized British society, with strong feelings of animosity between Leave and Remain supporters. This polarization has not diminished in the years since the referendum, and the ongoing debates over the implementation of Brexit continue to divide the country.

Brexit has also raised concerns about the future of the United Kingdom itself. In Scotland, where a majority of voters opted to remain in the EU, calls for a second independence referendum have grown louder. Northern Ireland, which has experienced disruptions due to the re-imposition of a customs border with the rest of the UK, has also seen renewed tensions, particularly with regard to the delicate balance maintained by the Good Friday Agreement.

Conclusion

The Brexit referendum is a prime example of how misinformation can shape public opinion and lead to profound political, economic, and social consequences. The Leave campaign's use of exaggerated claims, emotional appeals, and nationalist rhetoric created a narrative that resonated with voters, but it also distorted the reality of what Brexit would mean for the UK. As the economic and social costs of Brexit become increasingly apparent, it is clear that the lies and manipulation of information that characterized the referendum have left a lasting impact on the country.

Chapter 7:

Russian Interference: A Global Misinformation Campaign

In the modern geopolitical landscape, Russia has emerged as one of the most prominent actors in the use of misinformation as a tool of influence and manipulation. By leveraging digital platforms and exploiting political divisions in other countries, the Russian government has orchestrated a sophisticated global misinformation campaign that has influenced elections, destabilized democratic institutions, and sown distrust in the media. One of the most infamous examples of Russian interference occurred during the 2016 U.S. Presidential Election, but this campaign is part of a broader strategy that extends well beyond U.S. borders. In this chapter, we will examine how Russia has weaponized misinformation to achieve its geopolitical goals, drawing on interviews with cybersecurity experts from the FBI and CIA, as well as insights from the documentary *Active Measures*, which explores Russia's long-standing efforts to interfere in global affairs.

Russian Disinformation as a Geopolitical Strategy

Misinformation and disinformation have been integral components of Russia's geopolitical strategy for decades, rooted in the Soviet tradition of "active measures" (aktivnye meropriyatiya). Active measures include a range of influence operations, such as disinformation, propaganda, and psychological warfare, aimed at weakening adversaries by sowing discord, confusion, and distrust. These tactics were used extensively during the Cold War, but in the digital age, they have become even more potent.

Russia's disinformation campaigns are designed to exploit existing social, political, and cultural divisions within target countries. By amplifying controversial issues and circulating false or misleading information, Russian operatives aim to destabilize societies from within, eroding public trust in democratic institutions and fostering polarization. These efforts often go beyond electoral interference, encompassing a broader strategy of undermining Western alliances and promoting authoritarian alternatives to democracy.

Case Study: Russian Interference in the 2016 U.S. Election

The 2016 U.S. Presidential Election is perhaps the most well-known example of Russian interference through misinformation. The U.S. intelligence community concluded that Russia, under the direction of President Vladimir Putin, sought to influence the outcome of the election in favor of Donald Trump by conducting a widespread disinformation campaign. This campaign was primarily carried out by the Internet Research Agency (IRA), a Kremlin-linked organization based in St. Petersburg, which used social media platforms like

Facebook, Twitter, and Instagram to spread divisive content and misinformation.

The IRA created thousands of fake accounts posing as Americans, distributing content that inflamed political and social tensions on issues like immigration, race, and gun control. According to a 2018 report from the U.S. Senate Intelligence Committee, these efforts reached millions of Americans, with fake news stories and posts often going viral. One of the most striking examples was the creation of fake events, such as protests and rallies, that were promoted by Russian operatives but attended by real U.S. citizens, further demonstrating the effectiveness of these tactics in manipulating public opinion.

The scope of Russia's interference went beyond social media. Russian hackers, believed to be affiliated with the GRU (Russian military intelligence), also infiltrated the email servers of the Democratic National Committee (DNC) and released sensitive information through platforms like WikiLeaks. This operation, combined with the disinformation campaign, sought to discredit Democratic candidate Hillary Clinton and create doubts about the legitimacy of the election process.

While it remains unclear to what extent Russia's interference influenced the final outcome of the election, its impact on U.S. democracy was undeniable. The campaign deepened existing political divisions, undermined trust in the electoral process, and sparked ongoing debates about the vulnerability of democratic institutions in the digital age.

Insights from Cybersecurity Experts: The FBI and CIA on Russian Disinformation

To understand the full scope of Russia's disinformation campaigns, we turn to interviews with cybersecurity experts from the FBI and CIA who have studied Russian tactics in detail. These experts emphasize that Russia's approach to disinformation is both sophisticated and evolving.

"Russia has long seen disinformation as a low-cost, high-reward tool for achieving its strategic objectives," explains one former CIA officer who specialized in counterintelligence. "What makes the modern Russian approach so effective is its ability to adapt to new technologies, particularly social media. By leveraging these platforms, Russia can reach millions of people with minimal investment and create chaos without ever firing a shot."

According to an FBI cybersecurity expert, Russia's disinformation operations are highly coordinated and often involve multiple state actors working in tandem. "You have the Internet Research Agency running the social media campaigns, GRU conducting the cyberattacks, and Russian state media like RT and Sputnik spreading disinformation through more traditional channels. It's a full-spectrum approach aimed at influencing public opinion and destabilizing democratic governments," the expert explains.

These experts also highlight the challenges of combating Russian disinformation. "The biggest problem is that it's not just about fact-checking or removing false content," says the FBI officer. "Russia's goal is to create confusion, to make people distrust everything they see and hear. In that environment, even true information is called into question."

The Global Reach of Russian Interference

While the 2016 U.S. election brought Russia's disinformation efforts into the spotlight, similar tactics have been used across the globe. In Europe, Russia has been accused of interfering in elections and referendums in countries like France, Germany, and the United Kingdom. During the 2017 French Presidential Election, for example, Russian operatives launched a cyberattack against the campaign of Emmanuel Macron and spread disinformation aimed at undermining his candidacy. Similarly, in the run-up to the 2016 Brexit referendum, Russian bots and trolls amplified pro-Leave narratives, contributing to the spread of misinformation about the European Union and immigration.

Russia's interference extends beyond the West. In Ukraine, Russian disinformation has played a key role in the conflict over Crimea and the ongoing war in eastern Ukraine. Russian media outlets have pushed false narratives about Ukrainian forces committing atrocities, while social media campaigns have portrayed pro-Russian separatists as freedom fighters. This disinformation has been critical in shaping public opinion both within Ukraine and abroad, creating a distorted narrative of the conflict.

Russia's broader goal is to weaken NATO and the European Union by promoting nationalist and populist movements that oppose these alliances. By supporting anti-establishment candidates and parties, Russia seeks to fracture the unity of Western democracies and create a more favorable geopolitical environment for its own interests.

Active Measures: A Documentary on Russian Interference

The documentary *Active Measures* (2018) provides a detailed examination of Russia's global disinformation campaigns, tracing the history of these tactics from the Cold War to the present day. The film explores how Putin's government has used misinformation to manipulate elections, destabilize foreign governments, and advance its geopolitical agenda.

One of the central themes of *Active Measures* is the idea that Russia's interference in global politics is not a new phenomenon but rather an extension of long-standing Soviet tactics. The documentary traces the evolution of Russian disinformation from Soviet-era propaganda to the digital age, highlighting how Putin has modernized these techniques to exploit the vulnerabilities of Western democracies.

The documentary also includes interviews with key figures in U.S. intelligence, including former CIA Director John Brennan and former FBI Director James Comey, who discuss the challenges of countering Russian disinformation. Their insights reveal the complexity of combating a state actor that is willing to use deception and manipulation to achieve its goals.

Conclusion

Russia's use of misinformation as a tool of influence has had far-reaching consequences for global politics. From the 2016 U.S. election to ongoing conflicts in Europe, Russia's disinformation campaigns have undermined trust in democratic institutions, deepened political divisions, and advanced authoritarian interests. As we have seen, these campaigns are not isolated incidents but part of a broader strategy that seeks to weaken the West and reshape the global order. In the chapters to come, we will explore how other nations and actors have adopted similar tactics, contributing to the growing threat of misinformation to democracy worldwide.

Chapter 8:

Neo-Nazis in the Modern Age

The resurgence of Neo-Nazi movements in the 21st century is a disturbing development, revealing the persistence of extremist ideologies that many believed had been relegated to history. Far from being confined to the fringes, these movements have gained visibility, fueled by online communities, the rise of nationalist politics, and the spread of misinformation. This chapter explores the resurgence of Neo-Nazi groups, focusing on the 2017 Charlottesville "Unite the Right" rally as a case study. We will also hear from former white supremacists who have left the movement, as well as activists like Heidi Beirich of the Southern Poverty Law Center (SPLC), who work to combat hate and extremism.

The Resurgence of Neo-Nazi Movements

Neo-Nazi movements have their ideological roots in the violent, racist, and antisemitic doctrines of Adolf Hitler's Nazi Party. After the fall of Nazi Germany in 1945, these ideologies were widely condemned and marginalized. However, throughout the latter half of the 20th century, Neo-Nazi groups survived in pockets across the world, often blending their beliefs with other far-right or nationalist movements.

In the 21st century, the advent of the internet and social media has enabled Neo-Nazi ideologies to spread in new and alarming ways. Online platforms have allowed individuals with white supremacist and Neo-Nazi beliefs to organize, recruit, and amplify their message, often under the guise of free speech. This digital infrastructure has provided a global stage for the exchange of extremist propaganda, including conspiracy theories such as the "Great Replacement"—the false idea that white populations are being systematically replaced by non-white immigrants.

In the U.S., the resurgence of Neo-Nazi groups has coincided with broader trends in far-right politics, where grievances related to immigration, race, and nationalism have been exacerbated by misinformation and political rhetoric. Neo-Nazi movements have become intertwined with other extremist ideologies, including white supremacy and white Christian nationalism, creating a dangerous and volatile mix.

Case Study: The 2017 Charlottesville "Unite the Right" Rally

The 2017 "Unite the Right" rally in Charlottesville, Virginia, stands as a defining moment in the modern Neo-Nazi movement. What was ostensibly a protest against the removal of Confederate statues became a showcase for white supremacists, Neo-Nazis, and other far-right extremists, who gathered to promote their hateful ideologies under the banner of "heritage."

The rally was marked by overt displays of Neo-Nazi symbols and slogans, including swastikas, Nazi salutes, and chants of "Jews will not replace us." The event quickly descended into violence, culminating in the death of counter-protester Heather Heyer, who was killed when a white supremacist deliberately drove his car into a crowd. The violence in Charlottesville shocked the nation and forced a reckoning with the growing visibility of Neo-Nazi and white supremacist groups in the United States.

The Charlottesville rally was significant not only for its violent outcome but also for the way it highlighted the organizing power of Neo-Nazi groups in the digital age. Many of the participants were recruited through online platforms like 4chan, 8chan, and The Daily Stormer, which serve as breeding grounds for extremist rhetoric. These platforms allow individuals to radicalize, organize, and connect with like-minded people in ways that were not possible for earlier generations of extremists.

The response to Charlottesville, particularly from political leaders, further emboldened Neo-Nazi movements. When then-President Donald Trump said there were "very fine people on both sides," his words were widely interpreted as an attempt to equivocate between white supremacists and those protesting against hate. This perceived legitimization from the highest levels of government gave Neo-Nazi groups a sense of validation and momentum.

Interviews with Former White Supremacists

To gain a deeper understanding of how individuals are drawn into Neo-Nazi movements and, more importantly, how they can leave, we turn to interviews with former white supremacists who have renounced their hateful beliefs. Many of these individuals describe their initial attraction to Neo-Nazi ideology as rooted in feelings of alienation, anger, and a desire for belonging.

One former Neo-Nazi, who now works with organizations that help individuals exit hate groups, explained how his involvement began online. "I was looking for answers, and I found a community that made me feel like I belonged," he recalls. "They preyed on my insecurities and gave me a scapegoat—immigrants, minorities, Jews. They told me that white people were under attack, and I believed them."

He emphasizes the role that misinformation and propaganda played in reinforcing his beliefs. "When you're in that world, you're bombarded with so many lies that it starts to feel like the truth. I believed in things that now seem absurd to me—like the idea that there was a global Jewish conspiracy controlling the world."

Leaving the movement, he says, was a difficult and painful process. "It's not just about changing your beliefs; it's about rebuilding your entire identity. I had to confront the harm I caused and make amends. But it was worth it to break free from that hate."

The Role of Activists: Heidi Beirich and the Southern Poverty Law Center

Heidi Beirich, a long-time researcher and activist at the Southern Poverty Law Center (SPLC), has dedicated her career to tracking and combating hate groups in the United States, including Neo-Nazi movements. The SPLC's annual reports on hate groups have documented a sharp increase in the number of active Neo-Nazi groups in recent years, particularly following the election of Donald Trump in 2016.

Beirich attributes this rise to a combination of factors, including political rhetoric, online radicalization, and the normalization of hate speech. "What we've seen is a mainstreaming of extremist views that used to be confined to the margins," Beirich explains. "Neo-Nazi groups are using the internet to reach new audiences, and they're finding fertile ground in a political environment where racist and nationalist rhetoric is more accepted."

Beirich also points out the importance of monitoring and disrupting the financial networks that support these movements. "A lot of these groups rely on crowdfunding, merchandise sales, and donations to fund their activities. By tracking and exposing their financial backers, we can limit their ability to operate."

The SPLC's work is crucial in identifying and countering the activities of Neo-Nazi groups, but Beirich emphasizes that combating these movements requires a broader societal effort. "We need to address the underlying factors that drive people to these ideologies—economic insecurity, social isolation, and a lack of education about the dangers of hate. Only then can we hope to stop the spread of Neo-Nazi beliefs."

Conclusion

The resurgence of Neo-Nazi movements in the 21st century, as exemplified by events like the Charlottesville rally, is a sobering reminder that extremist ideologies are not relics of the past. These movements have adapted to the digital age, using online platforms to recruit and organize while exploiting political and social divisions. The rise of Neo-Nazism presents a serious threat to social cohesion and democratic institutions, and it demands a multifaceted response. By understanding the factors that drive individuals into these movements, as well as the tactics used to combat them, we can begin to address the root causes of hate and extremism.

Chapter 9

The Ideology of White Supremacy

W hite supremacy, an ideology rooted in the belief that white people are inherently superior to people of other races, has persisted for centuries. Though often associated with historical atrocities such as slavery and segregation, white supremacy has evolved and adapted to the modern world, finding new expressions and outlets. Today, it manifests in various forms, from far-right extremist movements to subtler forms of institutional racism. This chapter explores the roots of white supremacy and its modern manifestations, drawing on interviews with scholars like Kathleen Belew, author of *Bring the War Home: The White Power Movement and Paramilitary America*, and an examination of the infiltration of white supremacist groups into key institutions such as the military and law enforcement.

The Roots of White Supremacy

The ideology of white supremacy has deep historical roots, particularly in Western Europe and the United States. It was used to justify the transatlantic slave trade, the colonization of non-European peoples, and the displacement and extermination of Indigenous populations. In the United States, white supremacy provided the foundation for the institution of slavery, Jim Crow laws, and the systemic disenfranchisement of African Americans and other minority groups.

In the post-Civil War period, white supremacy took on an organized, violent form in the Ku Klux Klan (KKK), a terrorist organization that sought to maintain white dominance through intimidation, violence, and lynching. Throughout the 20th century, the ideology continued to thrive, despite civil rights advances, finding support in far-right groups opposed to racial equality and integration.

In the modern era, white supremacy has evolved beyond traditional groups like the KKK. Today, it encompasses a loose network of far-right movements, many of which have embraced new technologies and political opportunities to spread their message. From Neo-Nazis to white nationalist militias, these groups share a commitment to preserving what they perceive as the dominance of white culture and racial purity.

Modern Manifestations of White Supremacy

In recent decades, white supremacy has experienced a resurgence, driven by political, economic, and social forces. The election of the first Black U.S. president, Barack Obama, marked a significant milestone in racial progress, but it also triggered a backlash from those who felt threatened by changing demographics and the erosion of white dominance. This backlash has been characterized by the rise of far-right movements that explicitly embrace white supremacist ideologies.

One of the most notable manifestations of modern white supremacy is the rise of the "alt-right," a loosely affiliated movement that emerged in the 2010s. The alt-right blends white nationalism, anti-immigrant rhetoric, and a rejection of multiculturalism with internet-based activism. Its adherents promote ideas such as the "Great Replacement" theory, which falsely claims that white populations in Western countries are being systematically replaced by immigrants and people of color.

The alt-right, while initially dismissed as a fringe movement, gained mainstream attention during the 2016 U.S. Presidential Election, when it aligned itself with Donald Trump's campaign. White supremacist groups saw Trump's candidacy as a vehicle for advancing their agenda, viewing his rhetoric on immigration, crime, and nationalism as sympathetic to their cause. Trump's reluctance to fully disavow white supremacist support, most notably during the Charlottesville rally, further emboldened these movements.

Interview with Kathleen Belew: The White Power Movement and Paramilitary America

To better understand the modern resurgence of white supremacy, we turn to the work of Kathleen Belew, a historian and author of *Bring the War Home: The White Power*

Movement and Paramilitary America. Belew's research traces the development of the white power movement in the United States, particularly its transformation into a paramilitary force in the late 20th century.

In an interview, Belew explains how the white power movement became more militarized in the aftermath of the Vietnam War. "Many white supremacists were Vietnam veterans who felt alienated from mainstream society and disillusioned by the government. They brought their military training and experience into the white power movement, creating a paramilitary culture that embraced violence as a means to achieve their goals."

Belew notes that white supremacists have long viewed the U.S. government as an enemy, particularly after federal actions like the desegregation of schools and the passage of civil rights legislation. "These groups began to see themselves as soldiers in a race war, fighting against both the federal government and the perceived threat of racial integration."

In the 1980s and 1990s, white supremacist groups like the Aryan Nations and The Order engaged in a series of violent attacks, including armed robberies, bombings, and assassinations. These groups believed that their violent actions were necessary to overthrow the U.S. government and establish a white ethnostate.

Belew's work sheds light on how the white power movement has persisted and evolved, despite law enforcement crackdowns. "What's alarming is how these groups have managed to adapt and survive. They've moved into online spaces, where they can recruit new members and spread their propaganda without the same level of scrutiny they once faced."

The Infiltration of White Supremacist Groups into the Military and Law Enforcement

One of the most troubling developments in the resurgence of white supremacy is its infiltration into key institutions, particularly the military and law enforcement. Investigative journalism and government reports have revealed that white supremacists and other far-right extremists have sought to join these institutions to gain weapons training, access to intelligence, and positions of authority.

A 2019 report by the FBI identified the infiltration of white supremacists into law enforcement as a "persistent threat," warning that these extremists could use their positions to protect fellow members, sabotage investigations, and engage in acts of violence. Similarly, investigations by outlets like *The Intercept* and *ProPublica* have documented cases of police officers and military personnel being involved in white supremacist groups, including participating in violent rallies and sharing racist content on social media.

The presence of white supremacists in law enforcement has had serious consequences for public safety and trust in the police. In several high-profile cases, officers with known white supremacist affiliations have been involved in the use of excessive force against people of color. These incidents have further strained relations between law enforcement and minority communities, fueling calls for reform and accountability.

In the military, the presence of white supremacists has raised concerns about the potential for violent extremism among service members. A 2020 Pentagon report acknowledged that white supremacists and other far-right extremists were attempting to infiltrate the military to gain tactical training and build connections with like-minded individuals. The report called for increased screening and monitoring of service members to prevent extremists from using their military experience to further their ideological goals.

Conclusion

White supremacy, though rooted in historical injustices, remains a potent and dangerous ideology in the modern era. From the rise of the alt-right to the infiltration of key institutions like the military and law enforcement, white supremacist movements continue to adapt and evolve. As scholars like Kathleen Belew have shown, the white power movement is not just a relic of the past but a persistent threat to democratic institutions and social cohesion. Addressing this threat requires not only legal and political action but a deeper understanding of the roots and manifestations of white supremacy in contemporary society.

Chapter 10

White Christian Nationalism: A Theocratic Threat

W hite Christian nationalism has become a significant and increasingly visible force in U.S. politics, intertwining religious identity with white nationalism and far-right political ideologies. This movement seeks to impose a particular interpretation of Christianity on American life, while advancing exclusionary views on race, immigration, and cultural identity. White Christian nationalists envision the United States as a divinely favored nation that should be governed according to a specific set of Christian beliefs—often at the expense of religious freedom, pluralism, and democracy. In this chapter, we will examine the rise of white Christian nationalism, drawing on interviews with scholars Samuel Perry and Andrew Whitehead, authors of *Taking America Back for God: Christian Nationalism in the United States*. We will also explore the role of evangelical leaders in spreading nationalist ideologies and influencing the broader political landscape.

The Rise of White Christian Nationalism

White Christian nationalism is rooted in the belief that the United States was founded as a Christian nation and that its laws, culture, and identity should be shaped by conservative

Christian values. This movement fuses religious nationalism with racial and cultural anxieties, appealing primarily to white Americans who feel threatened by social and demographic changes. While Christian nationalism has long existed on the fringes of American politics, it gained renewed prominence in recent decades, particularly in response to the civil rights movement, the increasing visibility of LGBTQ+ rights, and the growing racial and religious diversity of the U.S. population.

One of the defining features of white Christian nationalism is its rejection of secularism and pluralism. Adherents believe that the United States should be governed by biblical principles and that Christianity—specifically a conservative, evangelical interpretation—should hold a privileged place in American life. This worldview often overlaps with far-right political ideologies, including white nationalism, which seeks to preserve white dominance in U.S. society.

The rise of white Christian nationalism has been fueled by a sense of cultural and political marginalization among white evangelicals, particularly as they perceive their values and beliefs to be under attack by secular forces. This sense of grievance has been amplified by political leaders, media outlets, and religious figures who frame issues such as immigration, abortion, same-sex marriage, and religious freedom as existential threats to the "Christian" identity of the nation.

Interview with Samuel Perry and Andrew Whitehead: The Christian Nationalist Worldview

In their book *Taking America Back for God: Christian Nationalism in the United States*, sociologists Samuel Perry and Andrew Whitehead analyze the roots and dynamics of white Christian nationalism. Their research reveals that Christian nationalism is not just about religion; it is about identity, power, and politics.

In an interview, Perry explains how white Christian nationalists view the United States as having a special covenant with God. "They see America as a divinely chosen nation, one that has strayed from its Christian roots and must be restored to its rightful place as a beacon of Christian virtue and authority," Perry says. "This vision often excludes non-Christians, people of color, and those who do not conform to traditional gender roles, as these groups are seen as threats to the 'purity' of the nation."

Whitehead emphasizes that Christian nationalism is not confined to the margins of society. "Our research shows that Christian nationalism is present across a broad swath of the American population, particularly among white evangelicals. It's not just fringe groups—it's a widespread ideology that influences how people view politics, immigration, and race," Whitehead notes.

The authors argue that Christian nationalism is deeply intertwined with a sense of white identity. "It's no coincidence that Christian nationalism is most prevalent among white Americans," Perry explains. "For many, the idea of a Christian nation is inseparable from the idea of a white nation. It's about preserving what they see as the true America—white, Christian, and male-dominated."

Evangelical Leaders and the Spread of Nationalist Ideologies

Evangelical leaders have played a significant role in legitimizing and spreading white Christian nationalist ideologies. Figures such as Jerry Falwell, Jr., Franklin Graham, and Robert Jeffress have promoted the idea that the United States is under siege by secularism, liberalism, and multiculturalism, and that Christians must reclaim the nation for God. These leaders have wielded significant influence over their followers, often framing political issues as part of a broader spiritual battle for the soul of the nation.

Jerry Falwell, Jr., the former president of Liberty University, was an early and vocal supporter of Donald Trump's presidential campaign, helping to galvanize evangelical support for Trump by portraying him as a defender of Christian values. Despite Trump's personal behavior and policies that many would consider at odds with Christian teachings, Falwell and other evangelical leaders saw him as a bulwark against the forces of secularism, liberalism, and globalism.

Franklin Graham, the son of the famous evangelist Billy Graham, has similarly positioned himself as a defender of Christian nationalism, frequently warning that the United States is turning away from God. In speeches and on social media, Graham has framed issues such as immigration, abortion, and religious freedom as part of a cosmic struggle between good and evil, encouraging Christians to fight for their beliefs in the political arena.

Robert Jeffress, pastor of the First Baptist Church in Dallas, Texas, has been one of the most prominent evangelical voices promoting Christian nationalism. In sermons and television appearances, Jeffress has called for the United States to return to its Christian roots, often portraying Islam, secularism, and progressive values as threats to the nation's future. His church has played a key role in mobilizing conservative Christian voters, particularly in support of Trump's presidency.

These evangelical leaders have not only spread nationalist ideologies but have also provided a theological justification for far-right political movements. By framing their political goals in religious terms, they have been able to mobilize large segments of the evangelical community to support policies that align with white Christian nationalist ideals.

The Political Influence of White Christian Nationalism

White Christian nationalism has had a profound influence on U.S. politics, particularly in the realm of immigration, religious freedom, and education. Adherents of Christian nationalism often advocate for policies that prioritize the interests of Christians—specifically white Christians—over those of other religious or ethnic groups.

One of the key policy areas where white Christian nationalism has had an impact is immigration. Christian nationalists often view immigrants, particularly those from non-Christian or non-white countries, as a threat to the cultural and racial identity of the United States. This view has shaped the rhetoric and policies of far-right political leaders, who have framed immigration as a crisis that threatens to "replace" white Christian Americans.

Christian nationalists have also pushed for laws that protect religious freedom in ways that privilege Christianity. This includes efforts to allow public displays of Christian symbols, restrict the rights of LGBTQ+ individuals, and ensure that Christian values are upheld in public schools. These efforts are often framed as a defense against secularism and the erosion of Christian influence in public life.

In education, white Christian nationalists have advocated for the teaching of creationism, the removal of LGBTQ+ content from curricula, and the promotion of "patriotic education" that emphasizes the United States as a Christian nation. These policies reflect a broader desire to control the narrative about America's history and identity, promoting a version of history that aligns with Christian nationalist beliefs.

Conclusion

White Christian nationalism represents a potent and growing threat to democratic values, religious pluralism, and racial equality in the United States. By fusing religious nationalism with racial identity, white Christian nationalists seek to reshape American society according to a narrow, exclusionary vision of Christianity. Scholars like Samuel Perry and Andrew Whitehead have shown how deeply embedded these beliefs are within American culture, particularly among white evangelicals, while evangelical leaders have played a key role in promoting and legitimizing these ideologies. As white Christian nationalism continues to shape U.S. politics, it poses a serious challenge to the principles of democracy, equality, and religious freedom.

Chapter 11:

The Role of Conspiracy Theories

C onspiracy theories have long been part of political discourse, but in recent years they have gained unprecedented traction and influence, particularly in the United States. Movements like QAnon, once a fringe internet phenomenon, have entered the mainstream and begun to shape political beliefs, behaviors, and even policy discussions. This chapter explores how conspiracy theories such as QAnon have gained political traction, with insights from experts like Mike Rothschild, author of *The Storm Is Upon Us*, and former QAnon believers who have left the movement. We will also analyze the psychological appeal of conspiracy theories and examine the political consequences of their widespread adoption.

How Conspiracy Theories Gain Political Traction

Conspiracy theories often thrive during periods of uncertainty, fear, and social upheaval. They provide simple, often sensational explanations for complex events, offering followers a sense of clarity and purpose. In the digital age, conspiracy theories can spread rapidly, amplified by social media algorithms that prioritize engaging content. This dynamic has enabled movements like QAnon to grow from obscure online communities to powerful political forces.

QAnon, in particular, is a conspiracy theory that emerged in 2017, claiming that a secret cabal of Satan-worshiping pedophiles controls global institutions and that Donald Trump was working to expose and defeat this elite group. Despite the absence of any evidence to support these claims, QAnon quickly gained a large and dedicated following, with its adherents believing in a coming "Great Awakening" and "Storm" in which the cabal would be exposed and punished.

What sets QAnon apart from many other conspiracy theories is its adaptability and inclusiveness. It is not a single narrative but rather an umbrella of interconnected theories that allow individuals to weave in their own beliefs and grievances. This flexibility has enabled QAnon to absorb other conspiracy theories, such as anti-vaccine sentiments, false claims of election fraud, and even older anti-Semitic tropes, further expanding its reach.

Political leaders have also played a role in legitimizing conspiracy theories. During his presidency, Donald Trump frequently retweeted QAnon-affiliated accounts and avoided condemning the movement, calling its followers "people who love our country." This tacit endorsement gave QAnon a level of legitimacy and emboldened its followers, who believed that they had the support of the president. The January 6, 2021, attack on the U.S. Capitol, in which many QAnon adherents played a prominent role, demonstrated the dangerous real-world consequences of conspiracy theories.

Interview with Mike Rothschild: Understanding QAnon's Appeal

To better understand how conspiracy theories like QAnon gain such powerful traction, we turn to Mike Rothschild, an investigative journalist and author of *The Storm Is Upon Us*, a comprehensive account of the rise of QAnon. Rothschild has spent years studying conspiracy theories, and his insights offer a critical perspective on how and why movements like QAnon resonate with so many people.

In an interview, Rothschild explains that conspiracy theories often gain followers by offering simple explanations for complex events. "People want to believe that there's a reason for the chaos and uncertainty in their lives, and conspiracy theories give them that. QAnon, for example, provides a black-and-white narrative where good is fighting evil, and it's very appealing to people who feel like they've lost control over their own lives."

Rothschild also points to the role of social media in spreading QAnon and similar conspiracy theories. "The algorithms on platforms like Facebook and YouTube are designed to keep users engaged, and unfortunately, conspiracy content is very engaging. It's sensational, it's emotionally charged, and it often plays into people's existing fears and biases. Once someone clicks on one QAnon video or post, the algorithms start serving them more of the same, creating a kind of echo chamber where the conspiracy becomes more and more entrenched."

When asked why QAnon attracted such a large following during the Trump presidency, Rothschild highlights the power of political endorsement. "When people see political leaders—even the president—refusing to condemn a conspiracy theory, it gives it credibility. Trump's refusal to denounce QAnon, combined with his amplification of conspiracy theories about the 'deep state' and election fraud, helped bring QAnon into the political mainstream."

Voices of Former QAnon Believers: The Road to Disillusionment

Understanding the psychology of conspiracy theories also requires listening to the stories of those who once believed but have since left the movement. Former QAnon followers describe a process of radicalization that often begins with seemingly innocuous content and escalates into a full embrace of the conspiracy.

One former QAnon believer, who became disillusioned after the failure of QAnon's predictions to come true, recalls how she initially became drawn to the movement. "I started following QAnon because I was frustrated with the political system and I wanted answers. At first, it was just interesting—something to read on the internet. But as I got deeper into it, I started believing in all of it. I thought I was part of something bigger, like I was helping to save the world."

The turning point for many QAnon believers came in the aftermath of the 2020 U.S. Presidential Election. QAnon had long predicted that Donald Trump would remain in office and that a mass arrest of "deep state" operatives would occur. When these predictions failed to materialize, some followers began to question the movement. "I waited for the 'Storm' to happen, but it never did," the former follower recalls. "It made me start questioning everything."

For others, the January 6 attack on the Capitol was the breaking point. The violence and chaos of the event shocked some QAnon believers, who had seen themselves as part of a righteous cause. "I never thought it would go that far," another former follower explains. "Seeing people storm the Capitol and realizing that QAnon had played a part in that—it made me realize that this wasn't about saving the country. It was about destruction."

The Psychological Appeal of Conspiracy Theories

At the heart of conspiracy theories lies a powerful psychological appeal. Conspiracy theories often provide a sense of certainty and control in a world that can feel chaotic and overwhelming. They offer followers an "inside" perspective, making them feel as though they possess secret knowledge that others do not.

Research by psychologists suggests that individuals who are drawn to conspiracy theories often share certain psychological traits. These may include a need for cognitive closure, a desire for certainty, and a tendency to see patterns and connections where none exist. Conspiracy theories also appeal to people's sense of identity, offering them membership in a community of like-minded individuals who share their grievances and beliefs.

The political appeal of conspiracy theories is equally significant. Conspiracies often blame societal problems on hidden forces or "elites," providing a convenient scapegoat for complex issues. In the case of QAnon, the conspiracy theory reinforced the idea that Donald Trump was fighting a corrupt establishment, giving his supporters a sense of purpose and justification for their political beliefs.

However, the political consequences of conspiracy theories are far-reaching and dangerous. By eroding trust in institutions, such as the media, the government, and the electoral system, conspiracy theories undermine democratic norms and fuel polarization. Movements like QAnon have led to real-world violence, as seen in the Capitol insurrection, and continue to pose a threat to public safety and democratic governance.

Conclusion

Conspiracy theories like QAnon have gained significant political traction by offering simplistic explanations for complex societal problems, exploiting psychological vulnerabilities, and being amplified by political leaders and social media platforms. As we have seen through the voices of former believers and experts like Mike Rothschild, conspiracy theories can have profound consequences not only for individuals but for entire societies. The spread of these dangerous narratives undermines trust in democratic institutions, promotes division, and, in extreme cases, leads to violence. In the chapters to come, we will further explore how misinformation and conspiracy theories intersect with extremist movements, and what can be done to combat their influence.

Chapter 12

The Global Spread of Nationalism and Misinformation

In recent years, nationalism has surged across the globe, with leaders in countries as diverse as Brazil, India, Hungary, and the Philippines riding waves of populist sentiment to power. Central to this rise of nationalism is the widespread use of misinformation—a powerful tool for these leaders to rally support, manipulate public opinion, and cement their authority. This chapter examines the global spread of nationalism, focusing on the role of misinformation in maintaining nationalist regimes. Through case studies on leaders like Jair Bolsonaro in Brazil and Narendra Modi in India, we will explore how misinformation has become a key strategy for nationalist movements, drawing on insights from political analysts and journalists who cover these regions.

The Rise of Nationalist Leaders and the Role of Misinformation

Nationalism, often defined as the belief that a particular nation's interests and culture are superior to others, has historically been associated with exclusionary politics, xenophobia, and authoritarian tendencies. Today, many nationalist leaders use misinformation to stoke fears of external threats—whether in the form of immigrants, religious minorities, or international organizations—and present themselves as defenders of national sovereignty. Misinformation allows these leaders to create a sense of crisis, mobilizing public support while vilifying opponents and dissenting voices.

One of the key features of modern nationalist movements is their reliance on populist rhetoric that portrays the leader as a champion of "the people" against corrupt elites, foreign influences, and unwanted outsiders. This narrative is often supported by disinformation campaigns that paint a distorted picture of reality, creating a political climate in which facts are fluid and truth is subjective.

Case Study: Jair Bolsonaro and the Politics of Misinformation in Brazil

Jair Bolsonaro, the far-right president of Brazil, provides a striking example of how nationalism and misinformation go hand in hand. Elected in 2018, Bolsonaro rode a wave of anti-establishment sentiment, fueled by fears of crime, corruption, and economic instability. His campaign made extensive use of social media, particularly WhatsApp, to spread false information about his opponents and inflate his own political accomplishments.

One of the most notorious examples of Bolsonaro's misinformation strategy occurred during the 2018 presidential campaign when fake news stories about his opponent, Fernando Haddad, went viral. These stories falsely claimed that Haddad's party was distributing "gay kits" to children in schools as part of a plan to indoctrinate them with leftist ideologies. Despite being thoroughly debunked, these stories were widely believed, shaping public opinion in Bolsonaro's favor.

Bolsonaro's misinformation tactics did not stop once he took office. Throughout his presidency, he has downplayed the severity of the COVID-19 pandemic, spreading false claims about the effectiveness of masks and vaccines, while promoting unproven treatments such as hydroxychloroquine. His refusal to follow scientific guidelines has had devastating consequences for Brazil, which became one of the hardest-hit countries during the pandemic. In addition to health misinformation, Bolsonaro has attacked the integrity of Brazil's electoral system, claiming without evidence that it is vulnerable to fraud—a narrative similar to that used by former U.S. President Donald Trump.

Despite the clear disconnect between Bolsonaro's claims and reality, his misinformation strategy has been remarkably effective. By framing his opponents as enemies of the people and positioning himself as a defender of national pride and traditional values, Bolsonaro has maintained a dedicated base of supporters, even in the face of widespread criticism and international condemnation.

Case Study: Narendra Modi and the Manipulation of Nationalism in India

In India, Prime Minister Narendra Modi has used nationalism and misinformation to consolidate power and promote the agenda of his Bharatiya Janata Party (BJP). Modi's rise to power in 2014 was fueled by promises of economic reform and a commitment to Hindu nationalism, which seeks to elevate the Hindu identity above India's other religious and cultural groups, particularly Muslims.

Modi's government, and its supporters, have used misinformation to portray Muslims as a threat to India's security and social fabric, fueling tensions between religious communities. A key example of this tactic is the spread of rumors and fake news about "love jihad," a baseless conspiracy theory that claims Muslim men are seducing Hindu women to convert them to Islam. This narrative has been amplified by BJP-aligned media outlets and social media networks, contributing to an atmosphere of fear and mistrust.

Misinformation has also been used to justify controversial government policies, such as the 2019 Citizenship Amendment Act (CAA), which fast-tracks citizenship for religious minorities from neighboring countries—except for Muslims. The law sparked nationwide protests, with critics arguing that it discriminates against Muslims and undermines India's secular constitution. In response, pro-government media outlets and social media platforms spread false claims about the protesters, accusing them of being anti-national and funded by foreign entities.

Modi has also capitalized on India's long-standing tensions with Pakistan, using misinformation to stoke nationalist fervor during military confrontations. In the aftermath of a 2019 airstrike against Pakistani militants, the Indian government exaggerated the success of the operation, claiming to have killed hundreds of terrorists—claims that were later disputed by independent reports. Nevertheless, the narrative of a decisive victory helped Modi bolster his image as a strong leader defending India's sovereignty.

Insights from Political Analysts and Journalists

To better understand the global rise of nationalism and the role of misinformation, we turn to interviews with political analysts and international journalists who have covered these movements. One political analyst, based in São Paulo, Brazil, explains that Bolsonaro's success can be attributed in part to the decline of traditional media and the rise of social media as the dominant platform for political communication. "Bolsonaro's campaign was a masterclass in using social media to bypass traditional media gatekeepers. By flooding WhatsApp with misinformation, his team was able to reach millions of voters with messages that traditional journalists couldn't fact-check in real-time."

In India, journalists covering Modi's government face significant challenges. One international correspondent based in New Delhi describes how independent media has come under increasing pressure. "There's a concerted effort to delegitimize any media outlet that challenges the government's narrative. Journalists who report on government corruption or the rise of Hindu nationalism are often branded as anti-national, and online harassment is rampant."

These analysts highlight a common theme: nationalist leaders rely on misinformation not only to win elections but to maintain power by discrediting opponents and controlling the flow of information. In countries like Brazil and India, where social media platforms dominate the political landscape, the spread of misinformation has created an environment where facts are increasingly difficult to discern.

The Global Spread of Nationalism: News and Studies

The rise of nationalist leaders is not confined to Brazil and India. Across the globe, from Hungary's Viktor Orbán to Turkey's Recep Tayyip Erdoğan, nationalist movements have gained ground, often fueled by misinformation that targets immigrants, minorities, and political opponents. These movements share a common strategy: they present themselves as defenders of the nation against external and internal threats, while using misinformation to create a sense of crisis and justify their actions.

Studies on the global rise of nationalism point to several key factors driving this trend. One major factor is economic inequality and the perception that globalization has left many people behind. Nationalist leaders exploit these grievances by blaming immigrants, refugees, and foreign governments for their country's problems. Misinformation about crime, job losses, and cultural decline is used to stoke fear and mobilize support for restrictive policies.

A 2020 report by the International Crisis Group found that nationalist leaders increasingly rely on social media platforms to spread their message, bypassing traditional media outlets and reaching voters directly. The report noted that nationalist movements often rely on misinformation to shape public opinion on issues like immigration, security, and national identity. In this environment, conspiracy theories and false narratives can gain significant traction, particularly among populations that feel disillusioned with mainstream politics.

Conclusion

The global rise of nationalism is a complex phenomenon, but one consistent factor is the use of misinformation to maintain political power. Leaders like Jair Bolsonaro and Narendra Modi have relied on disinformation to create narratives of crisis, stoke fears of outsiders, and frame themselves as the saviors of their nations. By distorting reality and manipulating public opinion, nationalist movements have gained a foothold in countries around the world, threatening democratic norms and institutions. As we explore further in this section, the consequences of these movements extend far beyond national borders, shaping global politics in ways that will be felt for years to come.

Chapter 13:

Misinformation and Immigration

Immigration has long been a contentious political issue, and misinformation has played a central role in shaping public opinion and policy. Across the globe, political leaders have used lies and distortions about immigration to stoke xenophobia, justify restrictive policies, and rally nationalist support. Misinformation about immigrants often centers on claims that they are responsible for economic decline, crime, and cultural change, despite substantial evidence to the contrary. In this chapter, we will examine how political lies have fueled anti-immigration sentiments, drawing on case studies from the United States, the United Kingdom, and Europe. We will also feature interviews with immigration lawyers and activists who are working to combat false narratives and humanize the debate around immigration.

How Political Lies Fuel Xenophobia and Anti-Immigration Policies

Misinformation about immigrants is often weaponized by political leaders seeking to gain or maintain power by exploiting public fears and insecurities. These false narratives typically frame immigrants as a threat to national security, economic stability, and cultural identity. By presenting immigrants as scapegoats for a host of social and economic problems, politicians can galvanize support for anti-immigration policies while deflecting attention from deeper systemic issues.

One of the most persistent lies about immigration is the claim that immigrants drain public resources and take jobs from native-born citizens. In reality, numerous studies have shown that immigrants contribute significantly to the economy, filling labor gaps, starting businesses, and paying taxes. However, the persistence of these false claims continues to fuel anti-immigration sentiment and shape public policy.

Another common falsehood is the association of immigrants with crime. Politicians and media outlets frequently claim that immigrants, particularly undocumented immigrants, are responsible for rising crime rates. However, studies have consistently shown that immigrants are less likely to commit crimes than native-born citizens. Despite this, the narrative of immigrants as criminals has become deeply embedded in political rhetoric, driving support for harsh immigration policies such as increased border security and mass deportations.

Case Study: Misinformation about Immigrants in the United States

In the United States, immigration has been a defining issue for decades, and misinformation has played a crucial role in shaping public perceptions. Under the Trump administration, misinformation about immigrants reached new heights, with the president repeatedly making false claims about immigrants, particularly those from Mexico and Central America.

One of the most infamous examples of this misinformation was Trump's assertion that Mexican immigrants were "bringing drugs, they're bringing crime, they're rapists." This characterization, which had no basis in fact, reinforced harmful stereotypes about Latin American immigrants and fueled anti-immigration policies such as the construction of a border wall and the implementation of the "zero tolerance" family separation policy.

Another key aspect of the misinformation campaign was the framing of asylum seekers as criminals. Trump and his administration frequently portrayed asylum seekers arriving at the southern border as dangerous criminals, despite the fact that the vast majority were fleeing violence and persecution in their home countries. This narrative justified the administration's harsh immigration enforcement measures, including the deployment of troops to the border and the indefinite detention of asylum seekers.

Misinformation about immigrants has also shaped public opinion on immigration policy. A 2019 Pew Research Center study found that nearly half of Americans believed that immigrants were more likely than native-born citizens to commit crimes—a belief that has been debunked by numerous studies. This false perception has contributed to widespread support for restrictive immigration policies, including the deportation of undocumented immigrants and the expansion of immigration enforcement agencies such as ICE (Immigration and Customs Enforcement).

Case Study: Misinformation and Brexit

In the United Kingdom, misinformation about immigration played a central role in the 2016 Brexit referendum, which saw the UK vote to leave the European Union. The Leave campaign, which advocated for Brexit, used misinformation about immigration to stoke fears about the impact of EU membership on British sovereignty, security, and culture.

One of the most widely circulated claims during the referendum campaign was the false assertion that Turkey was on the verge of joining the EU, and that millions of Turkish immigrants would soon flood into the UK. This claim, which was promoted in Leave campaign materials and speeches, played on xenophobic fears about Muslim immigrants and was designed to sway voters who were concerned about the impact of immigration on British society.

Another key aspect of the Brexit misinformation campaign was the claim that leaving the EU would allow the UK to "take back control" of its borders and reduce immigration. Pro-Leave politicians argued that EU membership had led to an uncontrollable influx of immigrants, particularly from Eastern Europe, and that Brexit would enable the UK to implement more restrictive immigration policies. This narrative, while appealing to voters concerned about immigration, ignored the economic benefits of immigration and the complex realities of the UK's labor market, which relies heavily on migrant workers.

The impact of this misinformation was profound. Many voters who supported Brexit did so because they believed that immigration was out of control and that leaving the EU was the only way to address the issue. In reality, immigration from non-EU countries had always been under the UK's control, and leaving the EU had little to do with reducing immigration from outside Europe.

Case Study: Immigration and Misinformation in Europe

Across Europe, misinformation about immigration has fueled the rise of far-right nationalist parties, many of which have used fearmongering about refugees and migrants to gain political power. In countries like Italy, Hungary, and France, political leaders have spread false claims about the supposed dangers of immigration, often linking immigrants to crime, terrorism, and cultural decline.

In Hungary, Prime Minister Viktor Orbán has been one of the most prominent figures in spreading anti-immigration misinformation. Orbán has repeatedly portrayed immigrants, particularly Muslim refugees, as a threat to Hungary's Christian identity and security. His government has launched campaigns claiming that immigrants are part of a plot orchestrated by the philanthropist George Soros to undermine Hungary's sovereignty. These claims, though baseless, have been effective in consolidating Orbán's political base and justifying his authoritarian policies, including the construction of border fences and the rejection of EU refugee quotas.

Similarly, in Italy, far-right leader Matteo Salvini has used misinformation to rally support for his anti-immigration agenda. Salvini, who served as Italy's interior minister, frequently claimed that immigrants were responsible for a rise in crime and that Italy's social services were being overwhelmed by migrants. These claims were used to justify policies such as the closure of ports to migrant rescue ships and the criminalization of NGOs that assist refugees. However, data consistently showed that immigration to Italy had decreased during Salvini's tenure, and that immigrants were less likely to commit crimes than native-born Italians.

Interviews with Immigration Lawyers and Activists

To understand how misinformation about immigration affects real people, we turn to interviews with immigration lawyers and activists who work on the front lines of the immigration debate. These experts describe the challenges they face in combating false narratives and advocating for the rights of immigrants in an increasingly hostile political environment.

One immigration lawyer based in the U.S. explains how misinformation impacts her clients. "The constant drumbeat of misinformation about immigrants being criminals or freeloaders creates a hostile environment for my clients," she says. "It makes it harder for them to access basic services, and it makes the public less sympathetic to their situation. We spend a lot of time just trying to correct falsehoods, whether it's in the media or in court."

Activists also emphasize the importance of humanizing the immigration debate. One activist working in Europe notes that the portrayal of immigrants as faceless threats has desensitized the public to the real struggles that refugees and migrants face. "People forget that behind every statistic is a person, often fleeing unimaginable violence and hardship. The misinformation campaign dehumanizes these people, turning them into political pawns."

Conclusion

Misinformation about immigration has had a profound impact on global politics, fueling xenophobia, justifying restrictive policies, and shaping public opinion. Case studies from the United States, the United Kingdom, and Europe demonstrate how political leaders have used falsehoods to stoke fear and manipulate voters. However, immigration lawyers and activists continue to push back against these narratives, working to humanize the debate and correct the distortions that have come to define the immigration conversation. As we move forward, it is essential to recognize the role that misinformation plays in shaping immigration policy and to challenge the lies that perpetuate division and fear.

Chapter 14:

Climate Change Denial: The War on Science

C limate change is one of the most pressing challenges of our time, yet the global response has been hampered by misinformation, denial, and political lies. For decades, powerful interests, including corporations, politicians, and media outlets, have engaged in a concerted effort to undermine the scientific consensus on climate change, casting doubt on the overwhelming evidence that human activity is driving global warming. This chapter will explore the political lies surrounding climate change, their global impact, and the forces behind climate denial. Through interviews with climate scientists like Dr. Michael Mann and activists like Greta Thunberg, we will examine how misinformation continues to obstruct meaningful action. Additionally, we will reference documentaries such as *An Inconvenient Truth* and studies on the economic consequences of climate misinformation.

The Roots of Climate Change Denial

Climate change denial did not emerge in a vacuum. For decades, fossil fuel companies, political leaders, and conservative think tanks have funded disinformation campaigns designed to sow doubt about the reality and causes of global warming. These campaigns have relied on tactics similar to those used by the tobacco industry to downplay the health risks of smoking, including the selective presentation of data, the promotion of contrarian experts, and the suggestion that more research is needed before definitive action can be taken.

One of the earliest and most influential examples of climate denial came from ExxonMobil, one of the world's largest oil companies. Internal documents revealed that Exxon scientists had known about the link between fossil fuels and climate change as early as the 1970s, yet the company spent millions of dollars funding organizations that promoted climate skepticism. This effort included the production of misleading reports and the support of so-called "experts" who downplayed the severity of global warming.

Climate denial was further amplified by conservative politicians and media outlets, particularly in the United States, where climate change became a partisan issue. Politicians with close ties to the fossil fuel industry, such as former Senator James Inhofe, famously called climate change a "hoax" and used their platforms to dismiss the findings of climate scientists. Right-wing media outlets, including Fox News, played a significant role in spreading misinformation about climate change, often framing it as an exaggerated or fabricated issue driven by liberal activists.

The Political Lies Surrounding Climate Change

The lies surrounding climate change take many forms, from outright denial of the phenomenon to more subtle forms of misinformation that question the extent of human responsibility or downplay the potential consequences. These lies have been used to delay climate action, protect corporate interests, and maintain the status quo.

One of the most persistent falsehoods is the claim that there is no scientific consensus on climate change. In reality, the overwhelming majority of climate scientists—97%—agree that human activity is the primary driver of global warming. However, climate denialists have repeatedly promoted the idea that the science is "uncertain" or "contested." This narrative has been reinforced by political leaders, particularly in countries with large fossil fuel industries, who argue that taking action on climate change would be premature or economically harmful.

Another common lie is the suggestion that climate policies will destroy jobs and cripple the economy. In fact, studies have shown that the transition to renewable energy has the potential to create millions of new jobs in sectors such as solar and wind power, while reducing the long-term economic costs of climate-related disasters. Nevertheless, opponents of climate action frequently use economic fearmongering to rally public opposition to policies such as carbon pricing, emissions regulations, and the Green New Deal.

The global impact of these political lies is profound. By delaying or obstructing climate action, misinformation has contributed to the worsening of climate-related crises, including rising temperatures, extreme weather events, and sea-level rise. Countries that are most vulnerable to climate change, such as small island nations and developing countries, bear the brunt of the consequences, despite being the least responsible for greenhouse gas emissions.

Interviews with Climate Scientists and Activists

To better understand the impact of climate misinformation, we turn to interviews with prominent climate scientists and activists who have been at the forefront of the fight against climate denial.

Dr. Michael Mann, a leading climate scientist and author of *The New Climate War*, has spent years combating climate misinformation. In an interview, Dr. Mann explains how climate denial has shifted over time. "In the early days, the focus was on denying the basic science of climate change—denying that the planet was warming or that humans were responsible. But as the evidence became overwhelming, the denial shifted. Now, it's more about deflecting blame, downplaying the risks, or promoting false solutions like geoengineering instead of reducing carbon emissions."

Mann also highlights the role of powerful corporate interests in perpetuating climate denial. "Fossil fuel companies have a vested interest in delaying the transition to renewable energy. They've spent decades funding think tanks, lobbying politicians, and spreading misinformation to keep their profits intact, even at the expense of the planet."

Greta Thunberg, the teenage climate activist who sparked a global movement with her school strike for climate, offers a powerful perspective on the generational impact of climate misinformation. "My generation is the one that will live with the consequences of the inaction caused by climate denial," Thunberg says. "The science is clear, but politicians and corporations are still refusing to act because they put short-term profits and power ahead of our future."

Thunberg's activism has brought attention to the urgency of addressing climate change, particularly through movements like Fridays for Future, which demand immediate and bold climate action. Her speeches, which call out world leaders for their failure to act, have been a stark reminder of the moral and ethical dimensions of the climate crisis.

The Economic Consequences of Climate Misinformation

The costs of climate change are already being felt across the globe, and the economic consequences of inaction are staggering. Studies have shown that delaying climate action will only increase the economic costs associated with climate-related disasters, including hurricanes, wildfires, droughts, and floods. According to a report by the National Bureau of Economic Research, if global temperatures rise by 4 degrees Celsius by 2100, the global economy could lose as much as 23% of its GDP.

In contrast, taking decisive action to reduce carbon emissions and transition to renewable energy could not only mitigate the worst effects of climate change but also create significant economic opportunities. The International Renewable Energy Agency (IRENA) estimates that the renewable energy sector could create over 42 million jobs by 2050. Moreover, investing in green technologies and infrastructure has the potential to stimulate economic growth, reduce energy costs, and improve public health.

However, climate misinformation continues to delay this transition. By promoting false narratives about the economic costs of climate action, opponents of environmental regulation have successfully slowed the implementation of critical policies. This delay increases the likelihood of more severe climate impacts in the future, which will be far more costly to address than if proactive measures are taken today.

An Inconvenient Truth and the Power of Documentary Storytelling

Documentary films have played a significant role in raising awareness about climate change and combating misinformation. One of the most influential films in this regard is *An Inconvenient Truth* (2006), directed by Davis Guggenheim and featuring former U.S. Vice President Al Gore. The film brought the issue of climate change into the mainstream, highlighting the scientific consensus on global warming and the urgent need for action.

An Inconvenient Truth was groundbreaking not only for its compelling presentation of climate science but also for its ability to shift public opinion. The film won an Academy Award and was credited with sparking renewed interest in environmental issues. However, it also faced backlash from climate denialists, who criticized the film's depiction of the science and labeled it as alarmist.

Despite this criticism, the film remains an important tool for educating the public about climate change and the dangers of inaction. It has been followed by numerous other documentaries, such as *Before the Flood* and *Chasing Ice*, which continue to raise awareness about the impacts of global warming and the misinformation campaigns that seek to undermine climate action.

Conclusion

Climate change denial represents a dangerous and deliberate war on science, fueled by powerful interests that prioritize profits and political power over the well-being of the planet. Through misinformation and lies, these actors have succeeded in delaying meaningful action on climate change, with devastating global consequences. As we have seen through the voices of climate scientists like Dr. Michael Mann and activists like Greta Thunberg, the time for denial and delay is over. The economic costs of inaction are staggering, and the longer we wait, the more difficult it will be to mitigate the worst effects of climate change. It is critical that we confront the political lies surrounding climate change and take bold action to secure a sustainable future for all.

Chapter 15:

The Pandemic of Misinformation

The COVID-19 pandemic not only unleashed a global health crisis but also gave rise to a parallel pandemic of misinformation—what the World Health Organization (WHO) has called an "infodemic." Lies, conspiracy theories, and false information spread rapidly, undermining public health measures, sowing distrust in science, and contributing to unnecessary deaths. This chapter explores how misinformation shaped the global response to COVID-19, featuring interviews with public health officials like Dr. Anthony Fauci and journalists who documented the crisis. We will also examine studies from the WHO on the extent and impact of the infodemic, drawing lessons for future public health challenges.

How Misinformation Shaped the Global Response to COVID-19

As COVID-19 spread across the globe in early 2020, misinformation about the virus spread even faster. From false claims about the virus's origins to misleading information about treatments and vaccines, the pandemic became a breeding ground for conspiracy theories and pseudoscience. These falsehoods not only confused the public but also undermined the efforts of governments and health authorities to control the spread of the virus.

One of the earliest and most persistent lies surrounding COVID-19 was the claim that the virus was a hoax or that its severity was being exaggerated for political purposes. This narrative gained traction in several countries, including the United States, where political leaders downplayed the threat of the virus and encouraged their supporters to disregard public health guidelines. The result was widespread confusion and reluctance to follow preventive measures such as wearing masks, social distancing, and getting vaccinated.

Misinformation about treatments for COVID-19 also became a significant problem. Unproven remedies like hydroxychloroquine and ivermectin were promoted as "miracle cures," despite a lack of scientific evidence to support their effectiveness. In some cases, these false claims were endorsed by political leaders and media figures, leading to dangerous consequences for those who took these drugs in place of seeking proper medical treatment.

Perhaps the most damaging form of misinformation during the pandemic was the campaign against COVID-19 vaccines. Anti-vaccine activists spread false information about the safety and efficacy of the vaccines, claiming that they caused severe side effects, altered DNA, or were part of a government or corporate plot to control the population. This misinformation led to vaccine hesitancy in many countries, slowing the global effort to achieve herd immunity and prolonging the pandemic.

Interview with Dr. Anthony Fauci: The Battle Against Misinformation

Dr. Anthony Fauci, Director of the National Institute of Allergy and Infectious Diseases (NIAID) and one of the most prominent public health figures during the COVID-19 pandemic, faced not only the challenge of managing the virus but also the constant flow of misinformation. In an interview, Dr. Fauci reflects on the difficulties of navigating the infodemic while trying to provide clear, science-based guidance to the public.

"One of the biggest challenges was the sheer volume of misinformation that was out there, particularly on social media," Fauci explains. "People were getting conflicting messages from all directions—some from credible sources, others from fringe figures or even political leaders who were downplaying the severity of the virus."

Fauci notes that the politicization of the pandemic made it much harder to get people to trust public health guidance. "When public health becomes a political issue, it's incredibly difficult to get people to listen to the science. You had one side saying, 'This is serious, and we need to take action,' and the other side saying, 'This is overblown, and it's all about control.' That kind of division leads to confusion, fear, and ultimately more deaths."

Dr. Fauci also addresses the challenge of combating vaccine misinformation. "The misinformation about vaccines was particularly harmful. We worked so hard to develop these vaccines in record time, and they were incredibly effective, but the lies and conspiracy theories about them created unnecessary fear. Convincing people to get vaccinated became a major hurdle because they didn't know who to trust."

Fauci emphasizes the need for better public communication strategies in future health crises. "We need to do a better job of getting accurate information out there quickly, but we also need to hold those who spread misinformation accountable. Lives are at stake, and we can't allow false information to undermine public health efforts."

The Media's Role in Covering the Misinformation Crisis

Journalists covering the pandemic were often on the front lines of the battle against misinformation, working to debunk false claims while reporting on the rapidly evolving health crisis. However, the media landscape itself became part of the problem, as certain outlets and personalities promoted conspiracy theories and misinformation, fueling distrust in public health measures.

In an interview, a journalist from *The New York Times* who covered the pandemic explains the challenges of reporting on COVID-19 in the face of an infodemic. "It was like trying to swim against the tide," she recalls. "Every day, we were bombarded with new misinformation—about the virus, about the vaccines, about masks. Our job was to separate fact from fiction, but the problem was that the fiction often spread faster and farther than the facts."

The journalist notes that social media platforms, in particular, played a key role in amplifying misinformation. "Facebook, Twitter, YouTube—they all became battlegrounds for the truth. While they made some efforts to remove or flag false information, the damage was often already done. People had shared it, believed it, and acted on it."

She also highlights the difficulties of holding those responsible for misinformation accountable. "There were so many bad actors—some spreading lies for political gain, others for profit. But the scale of the misinformation was so vast that it was hard to track it all down, let alone hold anyone accountable."

The WHO and the "Infodemic"

The World Health Organization (WHO) has been at the forefront of combating misinformation throughout the pandemic. In its efforts to address what it calls an "infodemic," the WHO has worked to provide clear, accurate, and timely information to the public, while also collaborating with social media platforms to curb the spread of false claims.

In a 2020 report, the WHO highlighted the ways in which misinformation about COVID-19 was undermining public health efforts. The report pointed out that false information spread faster and more widely than factual information, particularly on social media platforms. This misinformation often centered around conspiracy theories, such as the idea that the virus was created in a laboratory or that the pandemic was a hoax designed to impose government control.

The WHO's report also emphasized the need for greater media literacy among the public, noting that people who are better equipped to critically evaluate information are less likely to fall for misinformation. The organization has since launched initiatives to promote media literacy and fact-checking, aiming to improve the public's ability to discern credible sources from unreliable ones.

The Economic and Health Impact of the Misinformation Pandemic

The impact of COVID-19 misinformation was not limited to public health. The economic consequences of misinformation were also significant, as false narratives about the virus and vaccines prolonged the pandemic, disrupted global supply chains, and led to unnecessary lockdowns and restrictions.

In countries where misinformation about COVID-19 vaccines was particularly rampant, vaccination rates lagged, leading to higher rates of infection, hospitalization, and death. This, in turn, delayed economic recovery, as businesses remained closed and workers were unable to return to normal life. A study published in *The Lancet* estimated that hundreds of thousands of deaths could have been prevented if vaccine misinformation had not hindered immunization efforts.

Misinformation also had a devastating impact on vulnerable communities, particularly in low-income countries where access to accurate information and vaccines was already limited. In many of these regions, conspiracy theories about the virus and vaccines spread rapidly, exacerbating health inequities and prolonging the pandemic's economic toll.

Conclusion

The COVID-19 pandemic revealed the devastating power of misinformation in shaping public health responses and prolonging global crises. Lies and conspiracy theories about the virus, treatments, and vaccines undermined trust in science, fueled political divisions, and contributed to countless preventable deaths. As public health officials like Dr. Anthony Fauci and journalists covering the pandemic have noted, the battle against misinformation is as critical as the fight against the virus itself. The lessons learned from this infodemic will be essential in preparing for future health crises, as the global community works to ensure that truth, not falsehoods, guides our response to the challenges of tomorrow.

Chapter 16:

The Assault on the Press

A free and independent press is one of the cornerstones of democracy, serving as a watchdog that holds power to account, provides citizens with vital information, and fosters public debate. However, in recent years, political leaders across the globe have intensified their attacks on the media, seeking to delegitimize journalists, discredit fact-checking, and undermine the role of the press as a safeguard of democratic values. These efforts to erode trust in the media represent a serious threat to democratic institutions, as they weaken one of the essential mechanisms for accountability. In this chapter, we will explore how political leaders have assaulted the press, drawing on interviews with journalists from *The New York Times*, *The Washington Post*, and investigative outlets like ProPublica. We will also examine reports from organizations like Reporters Without Borders on the increasing dangers that journalists face in today's political climate.

How Political Leaders Have Attacked the Press

Throughout history, authoritarian leaders have sought to control or suppress the press to prevent scrutiny and maintain power. In recent years, this tactic has spread to democratic countries, where leaders have increasingly turned to public attacks on the media to delegitimize criticism and dismiss unfavorable reporting. By branding journalists as "enemies of the people" or accusing them of spreading "fake news," these leaders aim to erode public trust in the media and create an environment where truth becomes subjective and malleable.

One of the most high-profile examples of this assault on the press occurred during the presidency of Donald Trump. Throughout his time in office, Trump repeatedly attacked the media, labeling it the "enemy of the people" and referring to critical coverage as "fake news." These attacks were not just rhetorical; they were part of a broader strategy to undermine the credibility of institutions that provide oversight of the executive branch. Trump's hostility toward the media had a chilling effect on press freedom, contributing to an environment in which journalists were frequently harassed, threatened, and discredited for doing their jobs.

Trump's attacks on the press echoed tactics used by other nationalist and populist leaders around the world, from Brazil's Jair Bolsonaro to Hungary's Viktor Orbán and the Philippines' Rodrigo Duterte. These leaders, like Trump, have sought to control the narrative by demonizing the media, dismissing critical reporting as biased or false, and using state resources to promote their own narratives through sympathetic media outlets or state-run broadcasters.

Interviews with Journalists: Covering the Assault on the Press

Journalists from leading news organizations have found themselves on the front lines of this assault, working to maintain their integrity and hold power accountable in an increasingly hostile environment. In an interview with a senior editor at *The New York Times*, the impact of political attacks on the press was starkly described. "We've always had to deal with pushback from politicians, but what we've seen in the last few years is different," the editor explains. "Leaders are no longer just disputing our reporting—they're actively trying to discredit us as an institution, suggesting that the very idea of a free press is something to be distrusted."

Reporters from *The Washington Post* also shared their experiences of working in an environment where political leaders, particularly under the Trump administration, consistently attacked their credibility. "When you're labeled the 'enemy of the people,' it puts a target on your back," one reporter says. "We've seen a significant increase in threats, both online and in person, and it's not just from anonymous trolls—it's from people who genuinely believe that we're trying to undermine the country."

Investigative journalists at ProPublica have faced similar challenges, particularly when reporting on politically sensitive issues like corruption or misuse of power. "We've had to be incredibly careful in how we approach certain stories, knowing that the pushback could be severe," says one ProPublica reporter. "But our job is to follow the facts, no matter where they lead, and to hold those in power accountable, even when it's unpopular or dangerous."

These interviews reveal a common theme: political leaders are increasingly weaponizing distrust of the press to shield themselves from scrutiny and discredit legitimate reporting. In doing so, they undermine the public's ability to make informed decisions and weaken one of the most important institutions in a functioning democracy.

The Growing Dangers Journalists Face

The hostility toward the press has had tangible consequences, with journalists around the world facing increased harassment, threats, and even physical violence. According to Reporters Without Borders (RSF), the global environment for press freedom has deteriorated significantly in recent years. RSF's World Press Freedom Index, which ranks countries based on the level of freedom available to journalists, has documented a rise in attacks on journalists, both verbal and physical, as well as an increase in laws and regulations that restrict press freedom.

In countries like Hungary, Turkey, and the Philippines, governments have used a combination of legal pressure, financial coercion, and direct intimidation to silence critical journalists. In Hungary, Viktor Orbán's government has taken control of most of the country's media outlets, turning them into propaganda machines that promote the government's narrative while sidelining independent voices. Journalists who remain critical of the government face constant harassment, lawsuits, and in some cases, police raids.

In the Philippines, President Rodrigo Duterte has overseen a violent crackdown on the press, particularly targeting journalists who report on his controversial war on drugs. The case of Maria Ressa, founder of the news site *Rappler*, is particularly notable. Ressa has been arrested multiple times on dubious charges and has faced a barrage of threats and attacks from Duterte's supporters, both online and offline. Her case has drawn international attention, highlighting the growing dangers faced by journalists in countries where the government seeks to control the narrative.

In the United States, while press freedom remains robust compared to more authoritarian regimes, the environment has become more dangerous. Journalists covering protests, particularly during the Black Lives Matter movement and the January 6 Capitol insurrection, have faced violence, arrest, and intimidation from both law enforcement and protesters. These incidents reflect a broader decline in respect for the press and its role in a democratic society.

Reports from Organizations like Reporters Without Borders

Organizations like Reporters Without Borders, the Committee to Protect Journalists (CPJ), and Freedom House have been sounding the alarm about the global assault on the press. In its 2021 World Press Freedom Index, RSF reported that journalism is "completely or partly blocked" in over 130 countries, a stark indicator of the growing challenges faced by the media worldwide.

RSF's report also notes that the COVID-19 pandemic has exacerbated the situation for many journalists, as governments around the world used the crisis as a pretext to crack down on independent reporting. In countries like China and Russia, where press freedom has long been restricted, the pandemic provided an opportunity to further control the flow of information, with journalists who reported on government failures or COVID-related corruption facing arrest or censorship.

The rise of digital harassment, particularly through social media, has also created new challenges for journalists. Online harassment campaigns, often coordinated by political actors or their supporters, target journalists with threats, doxxing, and disinformation designed to discredit their work. Female journalists, in particular, have faced disproportionately high levels of online abuse, often of a misogynistic or sexual nature.

These reports underscore the importance of press freedom as a pillar of democracy, as well as the growing threats to journalists worldwide. The assault on the press is not just a concern for journalists—it is a broader attack on the public's right to know and to hold their leaders accountable.

Conclusion

The assault on the press is a direct attack on democracy itself. By discrediting the media and undermining public trust in journalism, political leaders are weakening one of the most important checks on power and eroding the transparency that is essential for a healthy democracy. The experiences of journalists from outlets like *The New York Times*, *The Washington Post*, and ProPublica, as well as the sobering reports from organizations like Reporters Without Borders, make it clear that the press is facing unprecedented challenges in an increasingly hostile environment. In the face of these threats, defending press freedom and the integrity of journalism is more important than ever.

Chapter 17

Elections Under Siege

E lections are the bedrock of democracy, providing citizens with a means to choose their leaders and hold them accountable. However, in recent years, misinformation campaigns have cast doubt on the integrity of elections, threatening the foundations of democratic governance. False claims of widespread voter fraud, electoral manipulation, and rigged outcomes have undermined public confidence in electoral systems and led to significant political instability. This chapter examines how misinformation has placed elections under siege, focusing on case studies from the United States, Brazil, and other democracies. Through interviews with election officials and cybersecurity experts like Chris Krebs, former director of the Cybersecurity and Infrastructure Security Agency (CISA), we will explore the real threats to electoral integrity and the dangerous consequences of false narratives.

How Misinformation Has Undermined Electoral Integrity

In recent years, misinformation about elections has become a powerful weapon used by political leaders and their supporters to sow doubt, delegitimize outcomes, and galvanize their base. By promoting false claims of election fraud, these actors seek to undermine the credibility of electoral processes and weaken public trust in democratic institutions. This erosion of trust can have long-term consequences, as citizens lose faith in their ability to affect change through the ballot box and turn to more extreme measures, such as protests, violence, or political disengagement.

The tactics used in election-related misinformation campaigns are varied, but they often follow a similar pattern: pre-emptively casting doubt on the integrity of the election before it even takes place, spreading false information about voting procedures or the counting process, and amplifying baseless claims of fraud once the results are announced. These narratives are often disseminated through social media, where they can spread quickly and reach large audiences before fact-checkers have a chance to respond.

The impact of election misinformation is profound. It not only destabilizes political systems but also polarizes societies, pitting citizens against one another and fueling distrust in the very mechanisms that ensure a peaceful transfer of power. Once the public loses faith in elections, the legitimacy of the government comes into question, creating fertile ground for authoritarianism and anti-democratic movements.

Case Study: Election Fraud Claims in the United States

The 2020 U.S. Presidential Election provides a stark example of how misinformation can undermine trust in electoral outcomes. In the months leading up to the election, then-President Donald

Trump and his allies repeatedly claimed, without evidence, that the election would be rigged, particularly if mail-in voting was widely used due to the COVID-19 pandemic. These claims were amplified through social media, right-wing news outlets, and partisan websites, creating an environment in which many voters already believed that the election could not be trusted.

After the election, in which Joe Biden was declared the winner, Trump and his supporters doubled down on their false claims of widespread voter fraud. Despite multiple recounts, audits, and court rulings confirming the integrity of the election, Trump continued to assert that the election had been stolen from him. This narrative culminated in the January 6, 2021, attack on the U.S. Capitol, where a mob of Trump supporters, many of whom believed the election had been rigged, attempted to overturn the results through violent means.

Chris Krebs, the former director of the Cybersecurity and Infrastructure Security Agency (CISA), played a key role in ensuring the security of the 2020 election. In an interview, Krebs reflects on the challenges posed by misinformation. "2020 was the most secure election in U.S. history, but the spread of lies about voter fraud put our entire democratic system at risk. The truth is that we have robust election security measures in place, but when political leaders tell their supporters not to trust the process, it undermines everything we've built to protect elections."

Krebs, who was fired by Trump after he publicly refuted the president's claims of election fraud, emphasizes the importance of transparency and factual reporting. "Misinformation thrives in the absence of clear, accurate information. As election officials, we have to be proactive in communicating with the public, explaining how elections work, and debunking false claims as quickly as possible."

The consequences of election misinformation in the U.S. are still being felt. Polls show that a significant percentage of Republicans continue to believe that the 2020 election was rigged, even though no evidence supports this claim. This enduring belief has led to efforts in several states to restrict voting rights, with proponents arguing that these measures are necessary to prevent fraud—despite the fact that voter fraud is exceedingly rare in the United States.

Case Study: Election Misinformation in Brazil

In Brazil, misinformation about elections has also posed a significant threat to democracy. President Jair Bolsonaro, a right-wing populist, has frequently cast doubt on the country's electoral system, particularly its electronic voting machines, which have been in use since the 1990s. Bolsonaro, who has drawn comparisons to Donald Trump for his confrontational style and disregard for democratic norms, has repeatedly claimed—without evidence—that the voting machines are susceptible to fraud.

In the lead-up to Brazil's 2022 presidential election, Bolsonaro ramped up his attacks on the electoral system, warning that the election could be stolen from him. These claims were widely circulated on social media, where Bolsonaro's supporters spread misinformation about supposed vulnerabilities in the electronic voting system. Despite reassurances from Brazil's Superior Electoral Court (TSE) and independent observers that the system was secure, Bolsonaro's false claims resonated with a large portion of the electorate.

When Bolsonaro ultimately lost the 2022 election to former President Luiz Inácio Lula da Silva, many of his supporters refused to accept the results, staging protests and calling for military intervention to overturn the outcome. While the situation did not escalate to the level of the January 6 insurrection in the U.S., the parallels were clear: misinformation about election fraud had severely damaged public trust in the democratic process and created the conditions for political instability.

In an interview, a Brazilian election official who worked with the TSE during the 2022 election expressed frustration with the prevalence of misinformation. "Our system is one of the most transparent and secure in the world, but once the president started claiming that it was rigged, it didn't matter what evidence we presented. People believed what they wanted to believe, and that made our job incredibly difficult."

The Global Threat: Misinformation in Other Democracies

The threat of election misinformation is not limited to the U.S. and Brazil. Across the globe, similar tactics have been used to undermine trust in elections and cast doubt on the legitimacy of democratic governments. In countries like Hungary, Turkey, and the Philippines, political leaders have employed misinformation to manipulate electoral outcomes, marginalize opponents, and weaken democratic institutions.

In Hungary, Prime Minister Viktor Orbán has used state-controlled media and social media platforms to spread false information about opposition parties, painting them as corrupt or as agents of foreign powers. This misinformation has helped Orbán maintain his grip on power, even as his government faces growing criticism from international organizations for its authoritarian tendencies.

In Turkey, President Recep Tayyip Erdoğan has similarly used misinformation to discredit his opponents and justify his consolidation of power. During recent elections, Erdoğan's government spread false claims about opposition candidates, accusing them of supporting terrorism or colluding with foreign enemies. These narratives were amplified by pro-government media outlets, helping Erdoğan secure electoral victories even as his popularity waned.

The use of election misinformation has also been documented in European countries like France and the United Kingdom, where far-right political movements have used false claims about voter fraud, immigration, and foreign influence to cast doubt on the legitimacy of electoral outcomes. These tactics have contributed to the rise of political extremism and the erosion of democratic norms across the continent.

The Role of Cybersecurity in Protecting Elections

As election misinformation continues to spread, cybersecurity experts like Chris Krebs are playing an increasingly important role in protecting the integrity of electoral systems. In his work at CISA, Krebs focused on strengthening election security by improving communication between federal, state, and local governments, as well as partnering with private-sector companies to defend against cyberattacks.

In an interview, Krebs emphasizes the importance of transparency and public engagement in building trust in elections. "The more open and transparent we can be about how elections work, the harder it becomes for misinformation to take hold. That means educating voters, explaining how votes are counted, and being upfront about the steps we take to secure the process."

Krebs also highlights the need for collaboration between election officials and social media platforms to combat the spread of misinformation. "Social media companies have a responsibility to address misinformation on their platforms. While we've seen some progress in terms of content moderation, there's still a lot of work to be done. We need to focus on stopping false claims before they go viral, and that requires a coordinated effort."

Conclusion

The global rise of election misinformation poses a grave threat to democracy. By casting doubt on the legitimacy of electoral processes, political leaders and their supporters are eroding public trust in one of the most fundamental aspects of democratic governance. As we have seen in case studies from the United States, Brazil, and other countries, the consequences of these lies are profound, leading to political instability, polarization, and even violence. The fight to protect elections from misinformation is ongoing, and it will require concerted efforts from election officials, cybersecurity experts, the media, and the public to ensure that democracy endures in the face of this growing challenge.

Chapter 18:

Misinformation and Political Violence

Misinformation and disinformation have not only distorted public understanding of key political issues but have also contributed to a rise in political violence. When lies and conspiracy theories spread unchecked, they can lead to the radicalization of individuals and groups, pushing them to take violent actions in defense of false narratives. The January 6, 2021, Capitol insurrection in the United States is one of the most striking examples of how political violence can be fueled by misinformation, but it is not an isolated incident. In this chapter, we will explore the relationship between misinformation and political violence, focusing on the events of January 6 as a case study. Through interviews with law enforcement officials and security experts who witnessed the radicalization of individuals through disinformation, we will examine the dangerous consequences of political lies.

How Misinformation Leads to Political Violence

Misinformation, particularly when it is politically motivated, can incite individuals to commit acts of violence. This is because false narratives often create a sense of urgency or crisis, leading people to believe that they must act decisively to prevent some perceived catastrophe. When political leaders and influencers spread lies about election fraud, government corruption, or other "threats" to society, they can radicalize their followers, pushing them toward violent resistance.

One of the most dangerous aspects of misinformation is its ability to dehumanize political opponents. When individuals come to believe that their adversaries are part of a grand conspiracy or are working to destroy the country, violence can be seen as a legitimate or even necessary response. This was a common theme in the events leading up to the January 6 Capitol attack, where supporters of Donald Trump were convinced that the 2020 election had been stolen and that it was their duty to "stop the steal" by any means necessary.

Misinformation can also erode trust in the rule of law and democratic institutions, leading individuals to believe that violence is their only recourse. When people are told that elections are rigged, that courts are corrupt, or that the media cannot be trusted, they may feel that the normal mechanisms of democratic governance are no longer effective, pushing them to take matters into their own hands.

Case Study: The January 6 Capitol Insurrection

The January 6 Capitol insurrection is a prime example of how misinformation can lead to political violence. In the months leading up to the event, former President Donald Trump and his allies repeatedly claimed that the 2020 U.S. Presidential

Election had been stolen through widespread voter fraud, despite the lack of evidence to support these claims. These false narratives were amplified by right-wing media outlets, social media platforms, and political leaders, creating a parallel reality in which millions of Americans came to believe that the election was illegitimate.

On January 6, 2021, thousands of Trump supporters gathered in Washington, D.C., for a "Stop the Steal" rally. As Trump gave a speech reiterating his false claims of election fraud, many in the crowd became convinced that drastic action was necessary to prevent Joe Biden from being certified as the next president. What followed was an unprecedented attack on the U.S. Capitol, as rioters stormed the building, assaulted law enforcement officers, and disrupted the certification of the Electoral College results.

The violence of January 6 was directly fueled by the misinformation that had spread in the months prior. Rioters carried signs and chanted slogans that reflected the false belief that the election had been rigged. Some of the most radicalized individuals, including members of far-right extremist groups like the Proud Boys and Oath Keepers, saw themselves as defending democracy from a corrupt system, even as they engaged in acts of sedition.

Interviews with Law Enforcement Officials and Security Experts

To gain a deeper understanding of how misinformation contributed to the radicalization of individuals involved in the January 6 insurrection, we turn to interviews with law enforcement officials and security experts who witnessed the events firsthand.

A Capitol Police officer who was on duty that day describes the moment when the peaceful protest turned violent. "It was clear from the beginning that many of the people in the crowd truly believed that they were there to save the country. They weren't just angry—they were convinced that they had no choice but to storm the Capitol because the election had been stolen from them. It was terrifying to see how deeply they believed the lies that had been spread."

The officer recalls how the rioters targeted specific lawmakers, chanting threats like "Hang Mike Pence" and searching for Speaker Nancy Pelosi. "They weren't just attacking a building— they were targeting the very people they believed had betrayed the country. That level of hatred and conviction doesn't come out of nowhere—it was stoked by months of misinformation and lies."

Chris Rodriguez, a former Homeland Security official and expert on domestic extremism, explains the role that disinformation played in radicalizing individuals ahead of the insurrection.

"What we saw on January 6 was the culmination of a long-term disinformation campaign that convinced people that their government had been stolen from them. The repeated lies about election fraud and government corruption created a sense of existential crisis for these individuals. When people believe that their democracy is being taken away, violence starts to seem like a justifiable response."

Rodriguez also emphasizes the importance of understanding the psychological impact of misinformation. "People who become radicalized by disinformation often feel like they are acting in defense of a higher cause. They're not just angry— they believe they're fighting for the survival of their country, their values, and their way of life. That makes it incredibly difficult to dissuade them from violent action because they see it as righteous and necessary."

The Global Threat of Misinformation-Driven Violence

The January 6 insurrection was not an isolated event. Around the world, misinformation has fueled political violence, from attacks on minorities to clashes between political factions. In Brazil, President Jair Bolsonaro's repeated claims of electoral fraud and corruption have led to violent protests and attacks on political opponents. In Myanmar, misinformation about the Rohingya Muslim minority fueled a genocidal campaign by the military, resulting in mass killings and displacement.

In countries like India and the Philippines, misinformation about religious or ethnic groups has contributed to mob violence and extrajudicial killings. These incidents demonstrate how the spread of lies, particularly those that dehumanize or demonize certain groups, can lead to widespread violence and destabilization.

Combating the Misinformation-Violence Nexus

As political violence fueled by misinformation becomes more prevalent, it is essential to understand the role that governments, social media platforms, and civil society can play in combating this dangerous phenomenon.

One critical step is holding political leaders accountable for the misinformation they spread. When politicians promote false narratives that incite violence, they must face legal, political, or reputational consequences. In the aftermath of January 6, several prominent figures were investigated or censured for their roles in spreading misinformation that contributed to the violence.

Social media platforms also have a responsibility to prevent the spread of disinformation. While companies like Facebook and Twitter have taken steps to curb misinformation by labeling false posts or banning certain accounts, experts argue that more aggressive action is needed. Algorithms that prioritize sensational or misleading content must be reformed, and stricter moderation policies should be implemented to prevent the viral spread of disinformation.

Finally, civil society organizations and community leaders must work to build resilience against misinformation. This includes promoting media literacy, encouraging critical thinking, and creating spaces for dialogue that can counteract the echo chambers in which disinformation thrives.

Conclusion

The link between misinformation and political violence is both clear and alarming. As seen in the January 6 Capitol insurrection, when false narratives take hold, they can lead to radicalization and violent action against democratic institutions. The challenge of combating political violence fueled by disinformation is complex, requiring a coordinated effort by governments, media platforms, and civil society. Understanding how lies and misinformation contribute to violence is essential for preserving democratic systems and preventing future acts of political extremism.

Chapter 19

The Global Attack on Human Rights

M isinformation is not only a tool for manipulating elections and stoking political violence but also a powerful weapon used by authoritarian regimes to erode human rights. By distorting reality, spreading falsehoods, and suppressing dissent, these regimes create environments where human rights violations can be committed with impunity. Vulnerable populations, including ethnic minorities, political dissidents, and marginalized communities, often bear the brunt of these disinformation campaigns, as they are framed as threats to national security or social stability. In this chapter, we will explore how authoritarian governments use misinformation to undermine human rights, drawing on interviews with human rights activists and UN officials. We will also examine case studies from China, North Korea, and Saudi Arabia, where political lies have had devastating consequences for human rights.

How Authoritarian Regimes Use Misinformation to Erode Human Rights

Authoritarian regimes rely on misinformation to control the narrative and justify human rights abuses. By monopolizing media channels, manipulating information, and spreading propaganda, these regimes create a false reality in which their actions are portrayed as necessary for maintaining security, order, and national unity. Misinformation is often used to dehumanize targeted groups, making it easier for governments to justify repressive measures, including mass surveillance, detention, and even violence.

A common tactic is to frame political dissidents, ethnic minorities, or opposition figures as threats to the stability of the state. This narrative is then disseminated through state-controlled media, social media platforms, and public speeches. By shaping public perception, authoritarian leaders can create the illusion that their harsh actions are protecting the nation from chaos or foreign influence, when in fact they are consolidating power and silencing dissent.

In many cases, authoritarian regimes use misinformation to obscure or deny human rights abuses. For example, governments may claim that reports of torture, extrajudicial killings, or forced disappearances are exaggerated or fabricated by foreign enemies or traitorous domestic actors. This strategy not only deflects blame but also weakens international efforts to hold these regimes accountable.

Case Study: China's Misinformation Campaign Against Uyghur Muslims

One of the most egregious examples of how misinformation is used to justify human rights abuses can be found in China's treatment of Uyghur Muslims in the Xinjiang region. Since 2017, the Chinese government has detained more than one million Uyghurs in what it calls "reeducation camps." These camps, which the government claims are designed to combat extremism and promote social cohesion, are in fact sites of widespread human rights abuses, including forced labor, indoctrination, and torture.

The Chinese government has engaged in a sustained misinformation campaign to justify its actions in Xinjiang. State media portray the Uyghurs as a dangerous, radicalized group that poses a threat to national security. Government officials have repeatedly denied allegations of human rights abuses, insisting that the camps are vocational training centers aimed at preventing terrorism. This narrative is further reinforced by tightly controlled media access to Xinjiang, where carefully orchestrated tours for foreign journalists and diplomats present a sanitized version of the reality on the ground.

International human rights organizations, including Amnesty International and Human Rights Watch, have documented extensive evidence of abuses in Xinjiang, but the Chinese government's disinformation campaign has made it difficult to hold the regime accountable. In interviews with UN officials, it is clear that the Chinese government's control of the narrative has impeded international efforts to address the crisis.

One UN official involved in human rights investigations describes the challenge of countering China's misinformation. "China has created a closed information loop in Xinjiang, where it controls the flow of information so completely that it's nearly impossible to get an accurate picture of what's happening. This allows the government to continue its abuses with little fear of international consequences."

Case Study: North Korea's Information Blackout and Human Rights Violations

North Korea represents an extreme case of how misinformation and information control can be used to shield a regime from scrutiny and perpetuate human rights abuses. The Kim family dynasty has maintained power for decades through a combination of state propaganda, repression, and a near-total blackout of external information. The North Korean regime's monopoly on information has enabled it to carry out widespread human rights violations, including forced labor, arbitrary detention, and extrajudicial killings, while preventing its citizens from learning about the outside world.

Misinformation in North Korea is not just a tool for controlling public perception—it is the very foundation of the regime's power. The government cultivates a personality cult around its leaders, portraying them as god-like figures who are infallible and benevolent. At the same time, the regime spreads lies about foreign countries, particularly the United States and South Korea, to create a sense of perpetual external threat. This narrative justifies the government's repressive policies, including mass surveillance and the militarization of society.

In interviews with defectors, it becomes clear how deeply the regime's misinformation shapes the lives of ordinary North Koreans. One defector, now a human rights activist, recalls how she grew up believing that North Korea was the most advanced and just country in the world. "We were taught from a young age that our leaders were protecting us from the evil outside world. We didn't know what human rights were because we didn't even have the vocabulary to talk about them."

The international community has struggled to address the human rights crisis in North Korea due to the regime's ability to control the narrative and isolate its population. Efforts by human rights organizations to document abuses are often thwarted by the regime's refusal to allow outside access and its disinformation campaign, which frames any criticism as part of a foreign plot to destabilize the country.

Case Study: Saudi Arabia's Misinformation and the Khashoggi Murder

Saudi Arabia's use of misinformation to cover up human rights abuses came into sharp focus with the 2018 murder of journalist Jamal Khashoggi. Khashoggi, a vocal critic of the Saudi government, was assassinated inside the Saudi consulate in Istanbul, a killing that the CIA later concluded had been ordered by Saudi Crown Prince Mohammed bin Salman. In the wake of Khashoggi's murder, the Saudi government engaged in a disinformation campaign to deflect blame and suppress the truth.

At first, the Saudi government denied any involvement in Khashoggi's disappearance, claiming that he had left the consulate safely. As international pressure mounted and evidence of Saudi complicity emerged, the government shifted its narrative, eventually admitting that Khashoggi had been killed but insisting that it was the result of a rogue operation. This misinformation campaign was supported by state-run media and pro-Saudi commentators, who sought to muddy the waters and create doubt about the regime's responsibility.

In interviews with journalists who covered the Khashoggi case, it is clear how effective the Saudi government's disinformation campaign was in delaying accountability. One reporter from *The Washington Post*, where Khashoggi was a columnist, describes the challenge of countering Saudi misinformation. "The Saudi government was extremely adept at controlling the narrative, both through its own media and by influencing foreign governments. It took months of investigation and leaks from intelligence agencies to piece together the truth, but by then, the damage had been done."

The Khashoggi case is a stark reminder of how authoritarian regimes use misinformation to protect themselves from the consequences of human rights abuses. Despite widespread international condemnation, Saudi Arabia has faced few tangible consequences for Khashoggi's murder, and the disinformation campaign has allowed the regime to continue its repressive policies with little fear of retribution.

Interviews with Human Rights Activists and UN Officials

Human rights activists and UN officials who work in regions where misinformation is used to justify abuses emphasize the importance of exposing the truth and holding regimes accountable. In an interview, a human rights activist who has worked extensively in China and Southeast Asia explains how misinformation undermines international efforts to protect vulnerable populations. "When governments control the narrative, they can commit atrocities without fear of consequences. The challenge is getting accurate information to the public and the international community so that these abuses can be stopped."

A UN official involved in monitoring human rights violations in authoritarian regimes echoes this sentiment. "Misinformation is one of the most effective tools for enabling human rights violations because it allows governments to operate in the dark. Our job is to shine a light on these abuses, but it's incredibly difficult when the government controls all the information."

Conclusion

Misinformation is a powerful weapon in the hands of authoritarian regimes, enabling them to commit human rights abuses with impunity. By controlling the narrative, these governments can justify repression, silence dissent, and evade accountability. Case studies from China, North Korea, and Saudi Arabia show how misinformation is used to obscure the truth and maintain power, often at the expense of vulnerable populations. Human rights activists, journalists, and international organizations continue to fight against this tide of disinformation, but the global attack on human rights will persist as long as authoritarian regimes are able to manipulate the truth.

Chapter 20:

Fighting Back: The Fact-Checkers

In an era where misinformation and political lies threaten the foundations of democracy, fact-checkers have emerged as critical defenders of truth. Journalists, researchers, and grassroots organizations are leading the charge to counteract falsehoods and provide the public with accurate information. Through rigorous investigations and public accountability, fact-checkers work to dismantle disinformation campaigns and restore trust in the democratic process. In this chapter, we will explore how fact-checking organizations such as Snopes, FactCheck.org, and others are fighting back against misinformation. We will feature interviews with the founders of these organizations, highlighting their strategies and successes, as well as case studies on effective debunking efforts.

The Rise of Fact-Checking in the Age of Misinformation

The explosion of misinformation in recent years, exacerbated by the rise of social media, has made it increasingly difficult for people to discern fact from fiction. Political lies, conspiracy theories, and misleading information circulate quickly, often with real-world consequences. In response, fact-checkers have stepped in to address this challenge by providing clear, evidence-based information to the public.

Fact-checking as a formal practice has grown rapidly in the 21st century, particularly in the wake of highly polarized elections, global health crises like COVID-19, and widespread disinformation campaigns. Organizations such as Snopes and FactCheck.org have become essential resources for individuals seeking to verify the accuracy of claims made by politicians, media outlets, and online influencers.

The fact-checking process typically involves scrutinizing statements for factual accuracy, cross-referencing information with credible sources, and publishing detailed explanations of how the claim was evaluated. Fact-checkers often address not only political statements but also rumors, viral social media posts, and even satirical content that may be misinterpreted as real news. This meticulous work is essential in combating the spread of false information, particularly in environments where political lies are used to manipulate public opinion.

Interviews with the Founders of Snopes and FactCheck.org

To better understand the role of fact-checkers in the fight against misinformation, we spoke with the founders of two of the most prominent fact-checking organizations: Snopes and FactCheck.org.

David Mikkelson, founder of Snopes, reflects on the evolution of the platform, which began as a small website focused on urban legends and hoaxes but has since grown into a leading authority on fact-checking. "When we started Snopes, it was more about debunking myths and folklore, but over time, we saw a huge shift toward political misinformation. The stakes became much higher when people started spreading dangerous lies about elections, health, and social issues," Mikkelson explains. "Our goal is to cut through the noise and give people a reliable source for checking facts, especially in a world where anyone can publish anything online."

Mikkelson emphasizes the importance of maintaining credibility and neutrality in the fact-checking process. "One of the biggest challenges is keeping people's trust. If they think we're biased or pushing an agenda, they'll dismiss our work. That's why transparency is key—we always show our sources, explain our reasoning, and correct any mistakes."

Brooks Jackson, founder of FactCheck.org, discusses the challenges of fact-checking in an era of hyper-partisanship. "There's a lot of pressure on us to take sides, but we're committed to being nonpartisan. Our mission is to hold both sides accountable, no matter how politically charged the environment becomes," Jackson says. "It's exhausting work, especially when misinformation is coming at us from all directions—politicians, social media, and even some mainstream news outlets. But we believe that by fact-checking, we can help reduce the spread of false information and give people the tools they need to make informed decisions."

Both founders highlight the importance of collaboration in the fight against misinformation. Fact-checking organizations work closely with social media platforms, news outlets, and educational institutions to flag false claims, correct the record, and promote media literacy. Partnerships with companies like Facebook and Google have enabled fact-checkers to reach wider audiences and slow the viral spread of false information.

Case Studies: Successful Fact-Checking Efforts

While the battle against misinformation is ongoing, there have been several high-profile successes in debunking political lies and disinformation campaigns. These victories demonstrate the power of fact-checking in counteracting falsehoods and holding accountable those who spread them.

Case Study 1: The "Pizzagate" Conspiracy Theory

One of the most infamous conspiracy theories of recent years was "Pizzagate," a baseless claim that linked a Washington, D.C., pizzeria to a supposed child trafficking ring run by prominent Democrats. The conspiracy theory spread widely online, fueled by anonymous posts on forums such as 4chan and Reddit. Despite having no basis in reality, the theory gained traction on social media and even led one armed man to storm the pizzeria in an attempt to "rescue" children he believed were being held there.

Fact-checking organizations quickly debunked the Pizzagate conspiracy, highlighting the complete lack of evidence and exposing the false connections that had been drawn between the pizzeria and political figures. Snopes and FactCheck.org, among others, played a crucial role in dismantling the theory, showing how the narrative had been concocted from misinterpretations, doctored images, and fabricated information. Although the damage was already done by the time the facts emerged, these efforts helped prevent further escalation and reduced the spread of similar conspiracies.

Case Study 2: COVID-19 Vaccine Misinformation

During the COVID-19 pandemic, misinformation about vaccines became rampant, contributing to vaccine hesitancy and undermining global public health efforts. False claims about the safety and efficacy of vaccines circulated widely on social media, with some conspiracy theorists suggesting that vaccines contained microchips, altered DNA, or caused infertility.

Fact-checking organizations, along with public health authorities, played a vital role in countering these lies. FactCheck.org partnered with the Annenberg Public Policy Center to provide real-time corrections of vaccine misinformation, while Snopes focused on debunking viral posts and rumors. By providing clear, evidence-based explanations of how vaccines work and addressing specific concerns raised by skeptics, these fact-checkers helped to combat vaccine hesitancy and reinforce the importance of following scientific guidance.

Case Study 3: The 2020 U.S. Election

In the aftermath of the 2020 U.S. Presidential Election, false claims of widespread voter fraud spread rapidly, particularly among supporters of Donald Trump. Despite numerous recounts and audits confirming the accuracy of the results, misinformation about "stolen" votes and rigged machines dominated right-wing media outlets and social media platforms.

Fact-checking organizations worked tirelessly to counter these false claims. FactCheck.org published detailed reports explaining how elections are conducted, why the fraud claims were baseless, and how the results had been verified by multiple independent sources. Snopes and other fact-checkers also debunked specific allegations, such as claims about voting machines switching votes or dead people voting, showing that these stories were fabricated or taken out of context. Although some segments of the population remained convinced of the fraud narrative, the fact-checking efforts played a key role in providing accurate information to the broader public and preventing further erosion of trust in the electoral process.

The Challenges and Future of Fact-Checking

While fact-checking has made significant strides in the fight against misinformation, it faces ongoing challenges. One of the most difficult aspects of the work is the sheer speed at which misinformation spreads, often outpacing the efforts to correct it. Social media algorithms prioritize sensational content, which can amplify false claims before fact-checkers have the opportunity to intervene.

Moreover, fact-checking alone is not always enough to change minds, especially in deeply polarized political environments where individuals may be more likely to believe information that aligns with their preexisting beliefs. This "backfire effect" presents a significant challenge to the fact-checking community, as individuals who are exposed to corrections may double down on their false beliefs rather than abandon them.

To address these challenges, fact-checkers are increasingly focusing on media literacy and education, teaching the public how to critically evaluate information and recognize misinformation when they encounter it. These efforts are essential in building long-term resilience to disinformation, as they empower individuals to become their own fact-checkers in a world where false information is ubiquitous.

Conclusion

Fact-checkers are playing a crucial role in the fight to protect democracy from the corrosive effects of misinformation. By holding political leaders, media outlets, and online platforms accountable for spreading falsehoods, fact-checkers help preserve the integrity of public discourse and provide the public with the tools they need to make informed decisions. As we look to the future, the continued success of fact-checking will depend on collaboration, innovation, and a commitment to truth in the face of relentless disinformation campaigns.

Chapter 21:

The Role of Education and Media Literacy

As the spread of misinformation becomes a global threat to democracy, the role of education in equipping individuals with the skills to critically evaluate information has never been more important. Media literacy—defined as the ability to access, analyze, evaluate, and create media in a variety of forms—has emerged as a critical tool in the fight against misinformation. By teaching people how to identify credible sources, understand the biases inherent in media, and discern fact from fiction, educators and advocates hope to inoculate society against the dangers of disinformation. This chapter explores the role of education and media literacy in combating the spread of misinformation, drawing on interviews with educators, media literacy advocates, and studies from institutions such as the Brookings Institution and Stanford University on the effectiveness of media literacy programs.

How Education Can Help Combat Misinformation

The educational system is uniquely positioned to play a transformative role in the fight against misinformation. From primary schools to universities, educators can integrate media literacy into curricula to empower students with the skills they need to navigate the complex media landscape. This includes teaching students how to verify information, understand the intentions behind different forms of media, and identify bias or manipulation in the news they consume.

One of the core challenges in combating misinformation is the fact that people are often unaware of their own cognitive biases, which can lead them to believe false information that aligns with their preexisting views. By teaching students to think critically about the information they encounter and question their assumptions, educators can help break down these biases and encourage a more thoughtful approach to media consumption.

Moreover, media literacy education is essential in developing the digital skills necessary to navigate the modern information ecosystem. In an age where misinformation is often spread via social media, fake news websites, and manipulated content, understanding how information is produced and disseminated is key to recognizing false or misleading narratives.

Interviews with Educators and Media Literacy Advocates

To better understand the importance of media literacy, we spoke with educators and media literacy advocates who are on the front lines of this effort. One educator, a high school teacher from New York, described the challenges she faces in teaching students how to evaluate information critically. "Many of my students get their news from social media, and they don't always stop to think about where that information is coming from or whether it's reliable," she explains. "Our job as educators is to teach them how to question what they see and think about the bigger picture—who's saying this, why are they saying it, and is there evidence to back it up?"

The teacher incorporates media literacy lessons into her history and social studies classes, where students are encouraged to analyze news articles, compare different sources, and look for signs of bias. "It's not just about spotting fake news," she says. "It's about teaching them to be skeptical and thoughtful consumers of information in general. That's a skill they can carry with them for the rest of their lives."

Dr. Renee Hobbs, a leading media literacy scholar and founder of the Media Education Lab at the University of Rhode Island, emphasizes the importance of early intervention in media literacy education. "By the time students reach high school, they've already developed habits around how they consume and interpret media," Hobbs notes. "We need to start teaching media literacy in elementary school, so kids grow up with a critical mindset toward the information they encounter."

Hobbs advocates for media literacy programs that are embedded across the curriculum, rather than being treated as a standalone subject. "Media literacy should be integrated into every subject area—whether it's history, science, or language arts—because the ability to critically analyze information is relevant to all areas of life."

Media literacy advocates like Hobbs also highlight the importance of teacher training. "Teachers need to be equipped with the tools and resources to teach media literacy effectively," she says. "That means professional development, access to up-to-date materials, and a strong support network."

The Effectiveness of Media Literacy Programs: Studies from Brookings and Stanford

The growing body of research on media literacy programs underscores their potential to significantly reduce the impact of misinformation. Several studies have demonstrated that students who receive media literacy education are better able to identify fake news, detect bias, and assess the credibility of information.

A 2018 study by **Stanford University's History Education Group** found that many students, even at the college level, struggled to evaluate the credibility of online information. The study highlighted the importance of teaching students how to analyze sources, particularly in an age where traditional media gatekeepers have been replaced by a vast array of digital content producers. In response to these findings, the group developed the **Civic Online Reasoning** curriculum, which has been widely adopted by schools across the United States. The program focuses on teaching students how to fact-check information, cross-reference sources, and understand the motives behind media production.

Research conducted by the **Brookings Institution** has also shown that media literacy programs can improve students' ability to discern fact from fiction. A 2020 report from Brookings emphasized the need for comprehensive media literacy education that goes beyond simply teaching students how to identify fake news. The report advocates for programs that foster critical thinking, encourage civic engagement, and promote digital citizenship.

One of the key findings of the Brookings study was that media literacy programs are most effective when they are tailored to the specific needs of the students they serve. For example, students in urban areas may encounter different types of misinformation than students in rural areas, and media literacy programs should reflect those differences. Additionally, the study found that hands-on, interactive approaches—such as fact-checking exercises, debates, and media production projects—were more effective than traditional lecture-based methods.

Case Studies: Successful Media Literacy Initiatives

Several media literacy programs around the world have demonstrated the potential of education to combat misinformation. These initiatives offer valuable lessons for how media literacy can be integrated into education systems to empower the next generation of informed citizens.

Case Study 1: Finland's National Media Literacy Program

Finland is widely regarded as a leader in media literacy education. The Finnish government has implemented a nationwide media literacy program that begins in primary school and continues through high school. Students are taught how to analyze news sources, recognize propaganda, and understand the impact of media on society. This early and sustained focus on media literacy is one reason why Finland consistently ranks at the top of global indices measuring resistance to misinformation.

In Finland, media literacy is not confined to the classroom. The government works closely with public broadcasters, libraries, and civil society organizations to promote media literacy for all citizens. This comprehensive approach has helped create a society where critical thinking and media skepticism are the norm.

Case Study 2: The United Kingdom's NewsWise Initiative

In the United Kingdom, the NewsWise initiative, developed by the Guardian Foundation, the National Literacy Trust, and Google, aims to teach primary school students how to navigate the news. The program provides free teaching resources to help

children develop skills such as identifying fake news,
understanding news bias, and creating their own news stories.

The program's interactive and engaging approach has been
praised for its effectiveness in helping young students grasp
complex concepts related to media and misinformation.
NewsWise also offers resources for parents and caregivers,
recognizing the role that family members play in shaping
children's media habits.

Case Study 3: The United States' Media Literacy Now

In the U.S., the organization **Media Literacy Now** has been at
the forefront of efforts to integrate media literacy into public
school curricula. The organization works with state legislatures
to pass media literacy education laws and advocates for the
inclusion of media literacy in state education standards. Several
states, including Washington, Illinois, and New Jersey, have
passed laws that require schools to teach media literacy, and
Media Literacy Now continues to push for similar legislation in
other states.

The organization's founder, Erin McNeill, emphasizes the
importance of legislative action in promoting media literacy.
"We can't leave it up to individual schools or teachers to decide
whether or not to teach media literacy—it needs to be a
fundamental part of every student's education," McNeill says.
"Our goal is to make sure that all students, regardless of where

they live, have access to the tools they need to navigate the media landscape."

Conclusion

Education and media literacy are powerful tools in the fight against misinformation. By teaching students how to critically evaluate the information they encounter, educators can help build a generation of informed citizens who are less susceptible to political lies and disinformation. The success of media literacy programs in countries like Finland, the U.K., and the U.S. demonstrates that these initiatives can make a significant difference in reducing the spread and impact of false information. As the global battle against misinformation continues, expanding media literacy education will be essential in ensuring that democracy can survive and thrive in the digital age.

Chapter 22:

The Path Forward: Reclaiming Truth in Politics

In an era marked by misinformation, disinformation, and political lies, restoring truth and trust in democratic institutions has become one of the most pressing challenges of our time. The erosion of trust in the media, government, and democratic processes has undermined social cohesion, contributed to political polarization, and weakened the foundations of democracy itself. However, history has shown that democracies can be resilient, provided that citizens, leaders, and institutions are committed to rebuilding the trust that has been lost. In this final chapter, we will explore what can be done to restore truth in politics, drawing on insights from political theorists, historians, and public figures who have studied democracy's resilience. Ultimately, the fight against misinformation requires collective action, as individuals, communities, and institutions work together to combat the age of lies.

What Can Be Done to Restore Truth and Trust

Reclaiming truth in politics requires a multifaceted approach that addresses the root causes of misinformation and distrust while strengthening the institutions that protect democratic integrity. Several key actions can help restore truth and rebuild trust in democratic systems:

1. **Strengthening Media Literacy and Critical Thinking**
   As we explored in the previous chapter, education plays a critical role in combating misinformation. By promoting media literacy and critical thinking skills from a young age, societies can equip individuals with the tools they need to identify falsehoods and evaluate information responsibly. This includes integrating media literacy into school curricula, encouraging public awareness campaigns, and providing resources for lifelong learning.
2. **Promoting Transparency and Accountability in Government**
   Transparency is essential for restoring trust in democratic institutions. Governments must take proactive steps to ensure that their actions are transparent and that citizens have access to accurate information. This includes publishing government data, ensuring freedom of the press, and creating independent bodies to investigate corruption and misconduct. Holding political leaders accountable for spreading misinformation is also key to restoring public trust. Legal and political mechanisms must be in place to penalize those who engage in disinformation campaigns.
3. **Reforming Social Media and Technology Platforms**
   Social media platforms play a significant role in the spread of misinformation. To address this, tech

companies must take greater responsibility for the content that is shared on their platforms. This can be achieved through stronger content moderation policies, collaboration with fact-checking organizations, and the use of algorithms that prioritize credible sources over sensational or misleading content. Governments should also consider regulations that require transparency in political advertising and disinformation campaigns.

4. **Building a Culture of Civic Engagement and Dialogue**
   One of the most damaging effects of misinformation is its ability to polarize societies and pit citizens against one another. Reclaiming truth requires fostering a culture of civic engagement and open dialogue, where people of differing views can come together to discuss issues based on facts. Community initiatives, town halls, and citizen assemblies can help bridge political divides and encourage constructive discussions.

5. **Empowering Independent Journalism**
   A free and independent press is crucial to holding power accountable and providing the public with factual information. Governments and civil society must protect press freedom and support independent journalism. This includes funding investigative journalism, ensuring the safety of journalists, and protecting media outlets from political and financial pressures that might compromise their integrity.

Interviews with Political Theorists, Historians, and Public Figures

To explore the resilience of democracy and the path forward in reclaiming truth, we spoke with several leading political theorists, historians, and public figures who have written extensively on the challenges facing modern democracies.

Steven Levitsky, co-author of *How Democracies Die*, emphasizes that misinformation is only one symptom of a broader democratic crisis. "Misinformation thrives in environments where institutions are weak and polarization is high," Levitsky explains. "Restoring truth requires rebuilding the guardrails of democracy—ensuring that political norms are respected, that institutions like the judiciary and the press remain independent, and that political leaders are committed to upholding democratic principles rather than undermining them for short-term gain."

Timothy Snyder, historian and author of *On Tyranny*, warns that the erosion of truth is often a precursor to authoritarianism. "When leaders attack the truth, they are attacking the very idea of accountability," Snyder says. "Without truth, there can be no shared reality, and without a shared reality, democracy cannot function. The battle to reclaim truth is really a battle to preserve democracy itself."

Greta Thunberg, the climate activist who has been outspoken in her fight against misinformation surrounding climate change, highlights the role of young people in leading the charge to reclaim truth. "We are the generation that will have to live with the consequences of today's lies," Thunberg says. "It's up to us to demand honesty from our leaders and to build a future based on facts and science, not deception."

David Mikkelson, founder of Snopes, offers a perspective from the fact-checking world. "Combating misinformation is a long-term effort, but it's not impossible. We've seen real progress when fact-checking is paired with education and public awareness campaigns. The key is persistence—truth doesn't always win the first battle, but over time, it can prevail."

Final Thoughts on the Need for Collective Action

Reclaiming truth in politics cannot be achieved by any one group or institution alone—it requires collective action from individuals, communities, governments, and the media. Every citizen has a role to play in this fight, whether it's by critically evaluating the information they encounter, holding their elected leaders accountable, or supporting efforts to improve media literacy in their communities. Democracy relies on informed citizens who can make decisions based on facts, not falsehoods.

At the same time, governments and technology platforms must take responsibility for their role in enabling the spread of misinformation. Policies that promote transparency, accountability, and the free flow of credible information are essential to restoring trust in democratic institutions. Social media companies, in particular, have a duty to address the ways in which their platforms have been used to amplify disinformation and sow division.

As we look to the future, it is clear that the fight against misinformation is far from over. However, by working together and taking decisive action, we can create a political culture where truth is valued, lies are exposed, and democracy can thrive.

References and Sources

Studies:

- **Pew Research Center**: Regularly publishes studies on public trust in government, media consumption, and the role of misinformation in shaping political opinions. Their reports on how disinformation impacts public perception are foundational for understanding the relationship between media and political attitudes.
- **Oxford Internet Institute**: Known for its research on the global impact of misinformation and disinformation campaigns, particularly how they spread on social media. Their studies offer in-depth analysis of the strategies used by political actors to manipulate information online.
- **Brookings Institution**: Brookings has published numerous studies on media literacy, the role of technology in spreading misinformation, and the effectiveness of policy interventions to combat disinformation.
- **Stanford University's History Education Group**: Their *Civic Online Reasoning* project focuses on teaching students how to evaluate digital information critically and has been instrumental in shaping media literacy education.
- **University Studies on Misinformation**: Various university-led research, such as studies on the

psychology of misinformation and the "backfire effect," provide a deeper understanding of why false beliefs persist even when confronted with factual corrections.

Documentaries:

- **The Social Dilemma**: This Netflix documentary explores the role of social media platforms in spreading misinformation and manipulating user behavior. It features interviews with former tech insiders and critiques the algorithms that prioritize engagement over truth.
- **Active Measures**: A documentary that details Russia's disinformation campaigns, including their interference in the 2016 U.S. Presidential Election. It explores the role of fake news, social media manipulation, and cyberattacks in modern geopolitical strategies.
- **Alt-Right: Age of Rage**: This documentary examines the rise of far-right extremism in the United States and the role that misinformation plays in radicalizing individuals. It juxtaposes the perspectives of white nationalists with those of anti-racist activists, providing a broader context of the social and political factors at play.
- **An Inconvenient Truth**: A groundbreaking documentary by Al Gore that brought the issue of climate change into the public spotlight. It addresses the misinformation spread by climate change denialists and the political obstacles to environmental action.

News Articles:

- **The New York Times**: Extensive reporting on misinformation, political extremism, and global disinformation campaigns. The Times has covered key events such as the January 6 Capitol insurrection, Russian interference in elections, and the spread of COVID-19 misinformation.
- **The Guardian**: Known for its investigative journalism, *The Guardian* has reported on global misinformation campaigns, including the role of tech platforms in spreading false information and the impact of disinformation on Brexit.
- **The Washington Post**: Provides detailed coverage of political misinformation in the U.S., including in-depth fact-checking of political leaders. Their "Fact Checker" column is a critical resource for debunking political lies.
- **ProPublica**: Investigative journalism that has exposed disinformation efforts related to elections, social media manipulation, and political corruption. ProPublica has also highlighted the growing threat of extremist groups fueled by misinformation.
- **Reuters**: A global news organization that has provided balanced reporting on the spread of misinformation worldwide, particularly during the COVID-19 pandemic and various elections across Europe and the Americas.

Interviews:

- **Academia**: Interviews with scholars such as Steven Levitsky (author of *How Democracies Die*) and Timothy Snyder (author of *On Tyranny*) provide critical insights into the erosion of democratic norms and the impact of misinformation on political stability.
- **Former Political Insiders**: Miles Taylor, former Department of Homeland Security official and author of *A Warning*, offers insider perspectives on how misinformation is used within governments to shape public opinion.
- **Journalists**: Interviews with prominent journalists like Maria Ressa (founder of *Rappler* in the Philippines) and reporters from *The New York Times* and *The Washington Post* provide firsthand accounts of the dangers faced by journalists in a world increasingly hostile to the press.
- **Former Extremists**: Individuals who have left extremist movements offer unique insights into how misinformation fuels radicalization and the processes through which people become de-radicalized.
- **Public Health Officials**: Dr. Anthony Fauci and other public health experts have provided critical perspectives on the "infodemic" surrounding COVID-19, emphasizing the role of misinformation in undermining public health efforts.
- **Election Experts**: Chris Krebs, former director of the Cybersecurity and Infrastructure Security Agency (CISA), offers expert analysis on how misinformation about elections can lead to real-world consequences, as seen

during the 2020 U.S. Presidential Election and subsequent Capitol insurrection.
- **Activists**: Interviews with human rights activists and advocates for media literacy provide insight into the grassroots efforts to combat misinformation and promote truth in public discourse.

These references and sources collectively provide the foundation for understanding the role of misinformation in modern politics and how various actors—journalists, activists, fact-checkers, and scholars—are working to combat its damaging effects.

The End

By
Mark A Conde